SERIES EDITOR: JOHN MOORE

ORDER OF BATTLE 9

THE ARDENNES OFFENSIVE

US VII & VIII CORPS and BRITISH XXX CORPS

CENTRAL SECTOR

BRUCE QUARRIE

First published in Great Britain in 2000 by Osprey Publishing, Elms Court, Chapel Way,
Botley, Oxford OX2 9LP United Kingdom
Email: info@ospreypublishing.com

ISBN 1 85532 858 5

Osprey Series Editor: Lee Johnson
Ravelin Series Editor: John Moore
Research Co-ordinator: Diane Moore
Design: Ravelin Limited, Braceborough, Lincolnshire, United Kingdom
Cartography: Chapman Bounford and Associates, London, United Kingdom
Origination by Valhaven Ltd, Isleworth, United Kingdom
Printed in China through World Print Ltd

00 01 02 03 04   10 9 8 7 6 5 4 3 2 1

FOR A CATALOGUE OF ALL BOOKS PUBLISHED BY OSPERY MILITARY, AUTOMOTIVE
AND AVIATION PLEASE WRITE TO:
  The Marketing Manager, Osprey Direct, P.O. Box 140, Wellingborough, Northants
  NN8 4ZA, United Kingdom. Tel. (0)1933 443863, Fax. (0)1933 443849,
  Email: info@ospreydirect.co.uk
  The Marketing Manager, Osprey Direct USA, PO Box 130, Sterling Heights,
  MI 48311-0130, USA. Tel. 810 795 2763. Fax. 810 795 4266.
  Email: info@ospreydirectusa.com

VISIT OSPREY AT www.ospreypublishing.com

Key to Military Series symbols

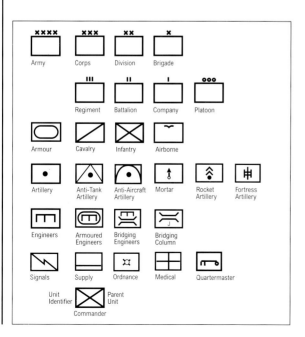

Army	Corps	Division	Brigade
Regiment	Battalion	Company	Platoon
Armour	Cavalry	Infantry	Airborne
Artillery	Anti-Tank Artillery	Anti-Aircraft Artillery	Mortar	Rocket Artillery	Fortress Artillery
Engineers	Armoured Engineers	Bridging Engineers	Bridging Column
Signals	Supply	Ordnance	Medical	Quartermaster
Unit Identifier	Commander	Parent Unit

Series style

The style of presentation adopted in the Order of Battle series is designed to
provide quickly the maximum information for the reader.

Order of Battle Unit Diagrams – All 'active' units in the ORBAT, that is those
present and engaged on the battlefield, are shown in black. Unengaged and
detached units, as well as those covered in previous and subsequent volumes,
are 'shadowed'.

Unit Data Panels – These provide a ready reference for all regiments,
battalions, companies and troops forming part of each division or battlegroup
and present during the battle, together with dates of attachment where relevant.

Battlefield Maps – In this volume, German units are shown in red and Allied
units in blue.

Order of Battle Timelines

Battle Page Timelines – Each volume concerns the Order of Battle for the
armies involved. Rarely are the forces available to a commander committed into
action as per his ORBAT. To help the reader follow the sequence of events,
a Timeline is provided at the bottom of each 'battle' page. This Timeline gives
the following information:

> The top line bar defines the actual time of the actions being described in that
> battle section.

> The middle line shows the time period covered by the whole action.

> The bottom line indicates the page numbers of the other, often interlinked,
> actions covered in this book.

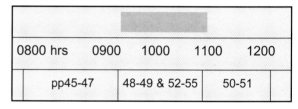

0800 hrs	0900	1000	1100	1200
	pp45-47	48-49 & 52-55	50-51	

Author's Acknowledgements

This book would not have been possible without the generous support of Bob
Kane, Chairman of Presido Press, Novato, California, for supplying and permitting
the use of material from Shelby L. Stanton's landmark book *World War II Order of
Battle* (1984). Captain (rtrd) Stanton has also been of considerable personal
help in the preparation of this volume, as has Mr Stuart Kohn of Maplewood, New
Jersey.

Editor's note

All individual battle maps are based on Government Survey 1:50,000 G.S. 4040
series dated 1938 and 1939, revised from aerial reconnaissance 1943, by
permission of The British Library.

CONTENTS

'ALL QUIET ... '

'Then out of the Mist ... '

On 15 December 1944 it was 'all quiet on the western front' – at least, in the Ardennes – and the GIs in their snow-covered fox holes surrounded by white-garbed pine trees were anticipating a peaceful Christmas. Ever since First Army had occupied the region in September/October and reached the West Wall, this had been the sector where nothing happened apart from some desultory shelling and the occasional brush with a German patrol. There had been heavy fighting in the north, at Aachen and Geilenkirchen and in the Hürtgen Forest, as well as to the south at Metz, but this part of Belgium and the Duchy of Luxembourg had become a backwater of the war.

Lieutenant-General Courtney Hodges, CO of First Army, was as grateful as any of his men for the respite, because he and they had fought long and hard since D-Day. This particularly applied to the 1st Infantry Division, which had landed at 'bloody Omaha' on 6 June and suffered nearly half the total D-Day casualties; to the 4th Infantry, which had come ashore on 'Utah' and captured Cherbourg; and to the 28th, which had endured the horrors of the Hürtgen Forest, losing 5,000 men in a fortnight. All three of these divisions in particular needed rest.

In addition, First Army's ranks had recently been swelled by the arrival of two fresh and untried infantry divisions, the 99th and 106th, which would benefit from having time to acclimatise before being thrown into the impending onslaught through the West Wall towards the Rhein planned for early in the New Year.

Like most of the higher-numbered divisions in the U.S. Army formed during 1942-43, these divisions had been used as manpower pools and, once they were trained, many of their men had been fed into other front-line divisions as casualty replacements. Before they shipped to Europe, the 99th and 106th had their numbers made up by 'press ganging' men from the USAAF or from anti-aircraft units. The result was that, when they arrived on the Continent, these divisions were only half trained and few of the officers knew their men really well.

Another result of the deceptive tranquillity of the Ardennes front was that many officers had been granted leave, which meant that when the German Volksgrenadiers began looming out of the pre-dawn mist on 16 December, some regiments, battalions and companies were led by officers more used to

The lull before the storm: GIs of the 28th Infantry Division enjoy local hospitality in Bastogne in September 1944. After their ordeal in the Hürtgen Forest, this is the sort of atmosphere (if not weather!) that the men on furlough were looking forward to over Christmas.
(U.S. Signal Corps)

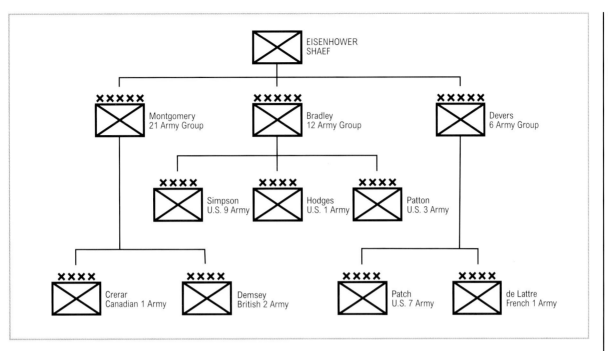

implementing orders issued from above than to initiating them. That most of them coped well, and several of them superbly, belies the common myth that American infantry were 'soft' and could not exist without candies, cookies and ice cream.

There was plenty of ice of a different sort in the steep, densely forested slopes of the Ardennes in December, making the narrow, tortuously twisting country roads impassable in places. Even 30-ton Sherman tanks could lose traction and slide into a ravine or slew sideways and block a road. Wheeled transport, even when snow chains were fitted, could only crawl cautiously at best. This would cause considerable delays after 16 December when units redeploying to meet the German threat were delayed for hours en route to their destinations. Fortunately, the same conditions slowed the advance of the Panzer divisions, seriously disrupting the German timetable and giving the Allies a short breathing space.

As the hours ticked down towards what the Germans called 'Null-Tag' (Day Zero), there were indications that something was afoot, but not all reports were passed upward and many were ignored. As a result, although some officers had premonitions of disaster, for the most part Allied intelligence discounted a major German push. The testimony of the occasional talkative prisoner was taken as Teutonic bragging. Reports of vehicle movements being heard in the middle of the night were ascribed to 'jitters'. There had been no aerial reconnaissance over this sector of the front since November and, although

a number of crack German divisions had 'disappeared' from sight, it was believed they were remustering in the Bonn-Köln region for a counter-attack through Roermond to recapture Aachen.

Nevertheless, if SHAEF remained inactive, further down the chain of command others were less sanguine. On 14 December, for example, the CO of the 4th Infantry Division, Major-General Raymond Barton, recalled all men on furlough to their units and had a precautionary conference with his regimental commanders on the 15th. But elsewhere, few preparations were taken and bored sentries peered blindly into the pitch-black night until, suddenly, at 0530 hrs on the 16th the horizon lit up with the flashes from hundreds of guns and heavy artillery shells began landing all along the thin line of foxholes. Then searchlights stabbed the air, their reflection from the clouds creating a ghostly moonlit effect, and the shadowy shapes of thousands of German infantry began emerging from the mist.

Pages 6–7: **Allied intelligence really did not know what opposed them east of the Schnee Eifel and river Our in December. Warnings of significant enemy troop movements tended to be disregarded because SHAEF expected no more than a spoiling attack in response to the Rur and Urft dams offensive in the north, and/or a response to Patton's impending attack in the Saar region further south. Recent claims that Eisenhower and Bradley deliberately left First Army's centre weak as bait in a trap are merely media 'hype'.**

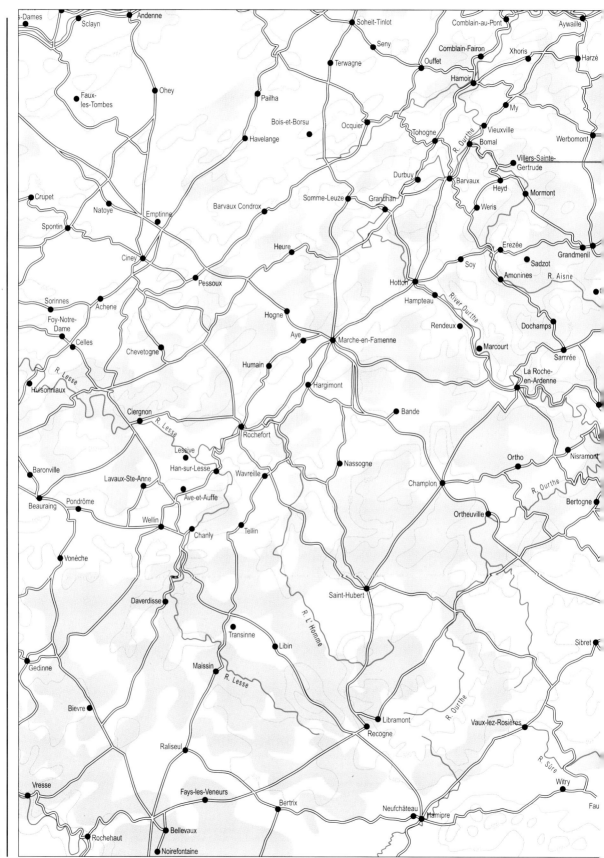

Francorchamps
Beverceé
Robertville
Elsenborn
La Gleize
umont
Malmédy
River Howarche
Rocherath
Bütgenbach
Waimes
R. Warche
CCB 9
Stavelot
Coo
R. Amblève
Bellevaux
Büllingen
Trois-Ponts
Ligneuville
Losheimergraben
Amblève
Losheim
Stadtkyll
XXX V
XXX VIII
14 V/VIII
Manderfeld
Recht
Meyrode
Grand-Halleux
Poteau
Schönberg
18 ?
Rodt
Lierneux
Vielsalm
St Vith
106 VIII
River Our
Salmchâteau
Bleialf
Bihain
Bovigny
Beho
Winterspelt
Prüm
Reuland
Habscheid
Gouvy
R. Ourthe Orientale
Lunebach
Houffalize
Troisvierges
? ?
Tavigny
Heinerscheid
River Clerf
Arzfeld
Bourcy
CCR 9
(-)
Clervaux
Marnach
Longvilly
Allerborn
Dasburg
Eschweiler
Hosingen
River Wiltz
28 VIII
Holzthum
Bitburg
Wiltz
Oberweis
Hoscheid
R. Sûre
Vianden
River Prüm
Tintang
CCA 9
Diekirch
4 VIII
Irrel
Beaufort
R. Sûre
Ettelbruck
River Sauer
rtelange
Echternach
0   5   10   15 miles
Osweiler
0   10   20 kilometres

7

U.S. FIRST ARMY

It was the misfortune of Courtney Hodges' U.S. First Army to bear the brunt of the German onslaught in the Ardennes, with its main weight falling on Major-General Troy Middleton's thinly spread 28th and 106th Infantry Divisions. The 99th Infantry Division of Major-General Leonard Gerow's V Corps on First Army's left flank was also hit hard by the strongest of the three attacking German armies, Sixth Panzer, but fortunately the 1st and 2nd Infantry Divisions were close at hand. The 30th Infantry Division, 'borrowed' from Lieutenant-General William Simpson's Ninth Army, was also brought into play and stopped 1 SS-Panzer

Lieutenant-General Courtney Hodges was a veteran of World War 1 who did consider the needs of his GIs and knew their lines were over-extended, but could do little to alleviate their precarious position until after the Germans struck.

(U.S. Signal Corps)

Division's drive west along the Amblève valley.

There were no such immediate reserves which could be rushed to the aid of Troy Middleton's hard-hit infantry, although each had a combat command from 9th Armored Division as a backstop. Hodges promptly recalled CCB from temporary attachment to V Corps and rushed it to St Vith, but that was all he could personally do to help Middleton other than appeal to 12th Army Group commander Omar Bradley for assistance.

Once the scale of the German offensive became apparent late on 16 December, Bradley reacted promptly to Hodges' request and ordered Simpson's 7th Armored Division to St Vith; this began arriving mid-afternoon on the 17th. It was already too late for two of the 106th Infantry Division's regiments which

---

U.S. FIRST ARMY
Lieutenant-General Courtney H. Hodges
Chief of Staff:
Major-General William G. Kean

V CORPS (Gerow)
VII CORPS (Collins)
VIII CORPS (Middleton)
  (to Third Army 20 December)
XVIII (AIRBORNE) CORPS (Gavin pp. Ridgway)
  (attached from SHAEF Reserve)
526 Armored Infantry Battalion
99 Infantry Battalion ('Norwegians')
740 Tank Battalion (Rubel)
  (C Troop detached to 30 Infantry Division)
741 Tank Battalion (Skaggs)
612 Tank Destroyer Battalion (Towed)
644 Tank Destroyer Battalion (M10) (Graham)
825 Tank Destroyer Battalion (M10)
143 Anti-Aircraft Artillery Gun Battalion (Mobile) (90mm)
413 Anti-Aircraft Artillery Gun Battalion (Mobile) (90mm)
51 Engineer Combat Battalion
158 Engineer Combat Battalion
299 Engineer Combat Battalion
300 Engineer Combat Battalion
1278 Engineer Combat Battalion
B Troop, 125 Cavalry Reconnaissance Squadron,
  Mechanized
9 Forestry Company (Canadian)
5 Fusilier Battalion (Belgian)
29 & II/118 Infantry Regiments (Lee)
  (duties included arresting deserters and black marketeers and
  covering Meuse river crossings south from Namur to Sedan)

---

were cut off in the Schnee Eifel and forced to surrender on the 19th. Bradley also alerted Simpson's 2nd Armored Division, and Ninth Army's 84th Infantry Division would also follow later. Similarly, Bradley

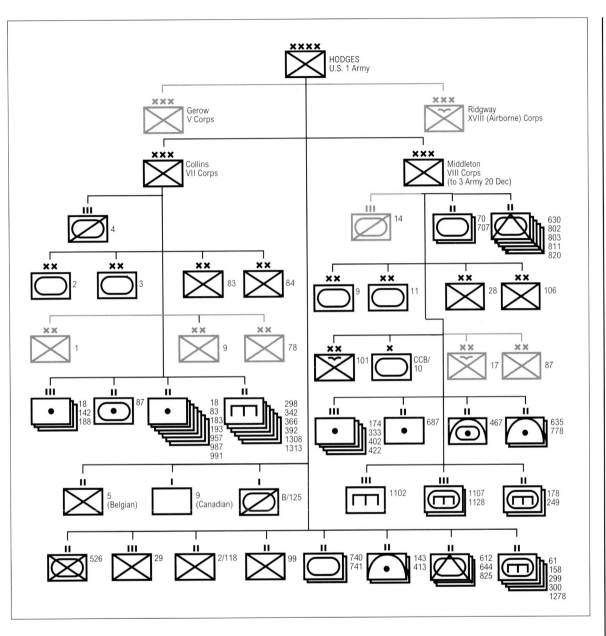

asked his Third Army commander, Lieutenant-General George Patton, for help, and CCB of 10th Armored Division arrived at the other critical road junction at Bastogne on 18 December.

Meanwhile, Eisenhower had reluctantly agreed to release the sole two divisions of SHAEF Reserve, the 82nd and 101st Airborne. The 82nd was deployed to Werbomont both to stop Kampfgruppe 'Peiper' from getting any further west, and to provide a safety net for the garrison of St Vith if evacuation proved neces-sary. Meanwhile, the 101st arrived at Bastogne on 19 December, in the nick of time to avert disaster.

All this while, Hodges and the other American commanders were merely reacting to German moves.

It was an emergency and there was little time to think beyond the present, but in the meantime the Germans were still pushing steadily west through the snow, sleet and fog which were keeping the Allied tactical air forces grounded. A new player now entered the field.

On D-Day, and up until 1 September, Field Marshal Bernard Law Montgomery had commanded all Allied ground forces. The increasing rift between him and Bradley in the end caused Eisenhower to remove Montgomery from overall command. Ever since, he had been chafing to regain control of U.S. forces, and the Ardennes crisis gave him the perfect opportunity.

Having said that, it did not take long for Eisenhower to see the sense of Monty's suggestion, relayed to him

The flash bulb is not kind to Lieutenant-General William Simpson (right) and most accounts of 'the Bulge' give him insufficient credit for his contribution towards the success of the counter-offensive. Seen with, from left, Bradley, Tedder, Eisenhower and Montgomery on 7 December, the third anniversary of Pearl Harbor. (U.S. Army)

after a meeting with Bradley in Verdun on 19 December. The weakness of the American position which Montgomery had spotted and which Eisenhower immediately recognised, was that Bradley, south of the new main battlefield, could not exercise competent control over the First, Third and Ninth Armies which constituted 12th Army Group. Communications between Bradley and Hodges, in particular, were insecure and unreliable, and likely to become more so the further west the Germans pushed. It would be much easier for Montgomery, comparatively closer to the action just over the border in Holland, to co-ordinate

First and Ninth Armies' response to the situation.

So, much to Bradley's and Hodges' disgust, Montgomery got his way and was given command of all ground forces north of the growing 'bulge', while Bradley retained Patton's Third Army, to which Middleton's VIII Corps was reassigned. Thus, First Army passed 'for the duration' to 21st Army Group.

While Hodges abhorred the idea of being subordinated to 'Monty', the field marshal did grasp the nettle firmly, even though his lack of social graces shocked Hodges' staff. The prompt re-alignment of VII Corps to guard the western flank, behind the river

---

U.S. INFANTRY RIFLE COMPANY*

Company HQ – 1 Captain, 2 Lieutenants (each 1 x .45 Colt automatic & 1 x .45 Thompson M1/M1AI or .45 M3/M3A1 SMG); 1 Technical Sergeant (SMG) & 27 men (2 x .30 HMG, 7 x .30 M1/M2 carbine & 20 x .30 M1 'Garand' rifle)

1st Rifle Platoon – Platoon Sergeant & 54 men (1 x 60mm mortar, 1 x .30 BAR & 3 x bazooka)
Section 1 –18 men (18 x .30 M1)
  Squad 1 – 9 men
  Squad 2 – 9 men
Section 2 (as above)
Section 3 (as above)

2nd Rifle Platoon – Three sections as above
3rd Rifle Platoon – Three sections as above

Weapons Platoon – Lieutenant and/or Sergeant)
Mortar Section – Sergeant & 9 men (2 x 81mm mortar, 1 x .30 M3 SMG & 9 x M1 carbine)

Machine-gun Section – Sergeant & 9 men (2 x .50 HMG, 1 x M3 SMG & 9 x .30 M1/M2 carbine)

*Note that the published TO&E (1942) was subsequently amended for European and Pacific theatres. This table is based upon U.S. Government Publishing Office Field Manual 7-20 of 1944 but with amendments to reflect a possibly more accurate picture of the situation in the Ardennes. It cannot be taken as either infallible or universal because many battalions and companies involved in the Ardennes were seriously under-strength (several at half strength or less, in fact), had lieutenants standing in for captains and sergeants standing in for lieutenants due to officers either being on leave (this being the 'quiet front') or casualty replacements ('reinforcements') not yet having arrived. Equipment levels also varied widely but reflect an average.

U.S. 'HEAVY' ARMORED DIVISION

(c. 14,488 men)

Division HQ (c. 164 men) & HQ Company (c. 138 men)

(3 x M5 Stuart or M24 Chaffee, 16 x M3 half-track, 3 x 57mm M1, 8 x .50 HMG, 10 x .30 LMG & 14 x bazooka)

COMBAT COMMAND A (HQ c. 100 men)

COMBAT COMMAND B (HQ c. 100 men)

COMBAT COMMAND R (No separate HQ – very ad hoc)

ARMORED REGIMENT (x 2) (c. 2,050 men)
HQ Company
I Medium Tank Battalion (c. 750 men)
HQ Company (1 x M4 [75mm])
A, B & C Companies (each 17 x M4 [75mm] & 2 x M4
[105mm])
II Medium Tank Battalion (c. 750 men)
HQ Company (as above)
D, E & F Companies (as above)
Light Tank Battalion (c. 550 men)
HQ Company (2 x M5/M24)
A, B & C Companies (each 19 x M5/M24)

ARMORED INFANTRY REGIMENT (c. 2,600 men)
HQ Company
I Battalion (c. 860 men)
HQ Company (1 x 81mm mortar, 1 x .50 HMG, 2 x .30 LMG &
2 x bazooka)
A, B & C Companies (each 1 x 75mm M3 GMC, 1 x 81mm
mortar M3, 18 x M3, 3 x 57mm M1, 3 x 60mm mortar,
12 x .50 HMG, 10 x .30 HMG, 6 x .30 LMG & 18 x bazooka)
II Battalion (c. 860 men)
HQ Company (as above)
D, E & F Companies (as above)
III Battalion (c. 860 men)
HQ Company (as above)
G, H & I Companies (as above)

ARMORED FIELD ARTILLERY BATTALION (x3)
(c. 540 men each)
HQ Company (2 x M3 half-track)
A, B & C Batteries (each 6 x 105mm M7 GMC & 10 x M3)

ARMORED RECONNAISSANCE BATTALION (c. 860 men)
HQ Troop (1 x M8, 2 x M3, 2 x .50 HMG & 2 x bazooka)
A, B & C Troops (each 14 x M8, 7 x M3, 1 x 81mm mortar
M3, 9 x 60mm mortar, 7 x .50 HMG, 18 x .30 LMG &
9 x bazooka)
Light Tank Troop (17 x M5/M24)
Support Troop (6 x 75mm M3 GMC)

ARMORED ENGINEER BATTALION (c. 690 men)
HQ Company (2 x M3, 2 x .50 HMG & 2 x bazooka)
A, B & C Companies (each 5 x M3, 6 x .50 HMG, 6 x .30 LMG
& 9 x bazooka)

ARMORED MEDICAL BATTALION (c. 415 men)
HQ Company
A & B Companies (each 2 x M3 ambulance & 3 x surgical
truck)

ARMORED SIGNAL COMPANY (c. 300 men)
(19 x M3, 13 x .50 HMG, 13 x .30 LMG & 24 x bazooka)

ARMORED MAINTENANCE BATTALION (c. 760 men)
HQ Company (1 x M3, 8 x .50 HMG, 4 x .30 LMG &
5 x bazooka)
A, B & C Companies (each 1 x M3, 10 x .50 HMG,
8 x .30 LMG & 10 x bazooka)

ARMORED SUPPLY BATTALION
(HQ Company c. 100 men)
(c. 35 x /– 2fi-ton trucks)

COUNTER-INTELLIGENCE CORPS DETACHMENT
(Data unavailable)

Ourthe, was purely Montgomery 'playing safe', as was his redeployment of his own XXX Corps to protect the line of the river Meuse. Major-General Lawton Collins' VII Corps, therefore, found itself as a new backstop for VIII Corps, while Matthew Ridgway's XVIII (Airborne) Corps found itself in a similar position for V Corps.

Montgomery was, by nature, a conservative strategist and tactician and, once it was clear soon after Christmas that the crisis was over, Hodges and his peers began to wonder when the Field Marshal would do something more positive than ensure the Germans did not get any further west than they already had. Eisenhower, too, chafed at Montgomery's inaction and began thumping the table in a gentlemanly manner. Eventually, suggestions for regaining the initiative proposed by VII Corps' commander Lawton Collins were

adopted for a counter-blow to take the pressure off the Bastogne corridor, retake St Vith, reunite First and Third Armies, and drive the Germans back where they had come from.

By this time, Hodges' First Army was in the mood for fighting back rather than falling back. His VII Corps was assembled, poised and raring to go, as was XVIII (Airborne). Middleton's VIII Corps, even though now part of Patton's Third Army, had survived the worst the enemy could throw at it and had been significantly reinforced. In warfare, a fortnight can be either an incred-ibly long or short time, and the speed of the Allied response to Operation 'Herbstnebel' had been everything Hitler's generals had feared. The Germans had sown the whirlwind; now it was Hodges' and Patton's chance to reap it with a vengeance.

U.S. FIRST ARMY

U.S. VII CORPS

Three days before Feldmarschall Walter Model launched Heeresgruppe B against the U.S. First Army's lines from Monschau in the north to Echternach in the south, Major-General Joseph 'Lightning Joe' Collins had his own VII Corps' forces arrayed to support V Corps' attack towards the Rur and Urft dams. The German onslaught brought a virtual stop to all offensive operations north of Monschau and within a few days would see Collins' corps redeployed en masse further south to cope with

Major-General Joseph Lawton Collins did not earn his nickname of 'Lightning Joe' in either Normandy or the Ardennes, as often assumed, but much earlier on Guadalcanal.
(U.S. Signal Corps)

the breakthrough in the Schnee Eifel and along the line of the river Our which had wreaked havoc amongst Troy Middleton's VIII Corps' infantry divisions – from north to south the 106th, 28th and 4th, backed up by the three combat commands of the 9th Armored Division.

The initial attack barely affected Collins' own troops directly. The 78th Infantry Division in the centre of his line was part of V Corps anyway, and manfully resisted the assault by 272 Volksgrenadier Division at Kesternich. To its north, the uncommitted 1st Infantry Division was rushed south to help the defenders south and west of Elsenborn ridge and reassigned to Major-General Leonard Gerow's V Corps. The 3rd Armored Division, which had been positioned to support the 78th Infantry, also moved south, part of it to complete the destruction of Kampfgruppe 'Peiper', and its other elements to Eupen and Hotton. They would shortly be joined by other units stripped from

---

U.S. VII CORPS
Major-General Joseph Lawton Collins
Chief of Staff:
Brigadier-General Williston Palmer

---

1 Infantry Division (Andrus)
  (to V Corps 16-19 December)
2 Armored Division (Harmon)
  (from XIX Corps 20-23 December)
3 Armored Division (Rose)
9 Infantry Division (Craig)
  (to V Corps 18 December)
78 Infantry Division (Parker)
  (from V Corps 18 December)
83 Infantry Division (Macon)
  (from XIX Corps 26 December)
84 Infantry Division (Bolling)
  (from XIII Corps 21 December)
4 Cavalry Group, Mechanized (MacDonald):
  4 & 24 Cavalry Squadrons, Mechanized
18 Field Artillery Group: 188, 666 & 981 Field Artillery
  Battalions
142 Field Artillery Group: 195 & 266 Field Artillery Battalions
188 Field Artillery Group: 172, 951 & 980 Field Artillery
  Battalions
18 Field Artillery Battalion
83 Field Artillery Battalion
87 (Armored) Field Artillery Battalion
183 Field Artillery Battalion
193 Field Artillery Battalion
957 Field Artillery Battalion
987 Field Artillery Battalion (-)
991 Field Artillery Battalion
298 Engineer Combat Battalion
342 Engineer General Service Regiment
366 Engineer General Service Regiment (Colored)
392 Engineer General Service Regiment (Colored)
1308 Engineer General Service Regiment
1313 Engineer General Service Regiment (Colored)

Lieutenant-General William Simpson's Ninth Army to the north, 7th Armored and 30th Infantry Divisions going to the newly arrived XVIII (Airborne) Corps, and 2nd Armored and 84th Infantry Divisions to VII Corps. Later, Collins' command would also be reinforced by the 83rd Infantry Division.

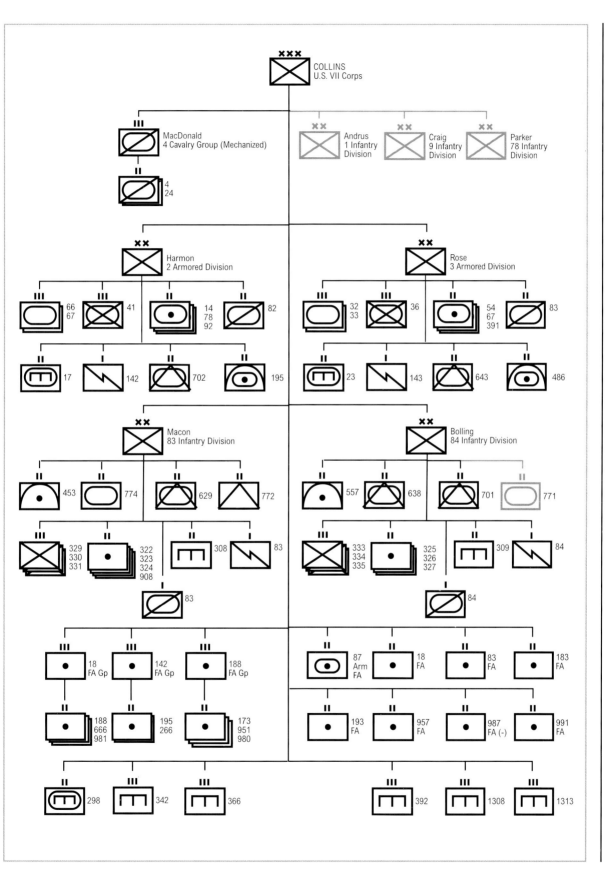

COLLINS
U.S. VII Corps

MacDonald
4 Cavalry Group (Mechanized)

4
24

Andrus
1 Infantry
Division

Craig
9 Infantry
Division

Parker
78 Infantry
Division

Harmon
2 Armored Division

66
67

41

14
78
92

82

17

142

702

195

Rose
3 Armored Division

32
33

36

54
67
391

83

23

143

643

486

Macon
83 Infantry Division

453

774

629

772

329
330
331

322
323
324
908

308

83

83

Bolling
84 Infantry Division

557

638

701

771

333
334
335

325
326
327

309

84

84

18
FA Gp

142
FA Gp

188
FA Gp

87
Arm
FA

18
FA

83
FA

183
FA

188
666
981

195
266

173
951
980

193
FA

957
FA

987
FA (-)

991
FA

298

342

366

392

1308

1313

U.S. VII CORPS TROOPS

4 Cavalry Group (c. 1,500 men)
Group HQ and HQ Troop

4 & 24 Cavalry Reconnaissance Squadrons, Mechanized
HQ Troop (4 x M8, 2 x M3, 1 x .50 HMG & 1 x bazooka)
A, B & C Troops (each 12 x M8, 8 x M3, 1 x 81mm mortar,
  9 x 60mm mortar, 8 x .50 HMG, 18 x .30 LMG &
  10 x bazooka)
Light Tank Troop (17 x M5/M24)
Support Troop (6 x 75mm M3 GMC)

18 Field Artillery Group

188 Field Artillery Battalion (12 x 155mm M1 gun,
  tractor-drawn)
666 Field Artillery Battalion (12 x 155mm M1A1 howitzer,
  tractor-drawn)
981 Field Artillery Battalion (12 x 155mm M1 gun,
  truck-drawn)

142 Field Artillery Group

195 Field Artillery Battalion (12 x 8" M1 howitzer, tractor-
drawn)
266 Field Artillery Battalion (6 x 240mm M1 howitzer,
  tractor-drawn)

188 Field Artillery Group

172 Field Artillery Battalion (12 x 4.5" M1 gun, tractor-drawn)
951 Field Artillery Battalion (12 x 155mm M1A1 howitzer,
  tractor-drawn)
980 Field Artillery Battalion (12 x 155mm M1 gun,
  truck-drawn)

Field Artillery Battalions

18 (12 x 105mm M2A1 howitzer, truck-drawn)
83 (data unavailable, believed 12 x 105mm M2A1
  howitzer, truck-drawn)
87 (despite being designated 'Armored' in 1942,
  12 x 105mm M2A1 howitzer, truck-drawn)
183 (12 x 155mm M1Al howitzer, tractor-drawn)
193 (12 x 105mm M2A1 howitzer, truck-drawn)
957 (12 x 155mm M1A1 howitzer, tractor-drawn)
987 (6 x 155mm M12 GMC)
991 (12 x155mm M12 GMC)

The architects of First Army's eventual victory in the northern sector of 'the Bulge'. From right, XVIII (Airborne) Corps' CO Matthew Ridgway, Field Marshal Bernard Law Montgomery and VII Corps' commander Joe Collins. It was, of course, 'Monty' who claimed the credit, for which he was publicly censured and nearly sacked. (U.S. Signal Corps)

nickname while commanding the 25th 'Tropic Lightning' Infantry Division on Guadalcanal and New Georgia in 1942-43. In January 1944 he was given command of VII Corps, and on 6 June had the satisfaction of getting the whole of the 4th Infantry Division ashore across 'Utah' beach by midnight; its leading regiment, the 8th, had suffered just 12 fatalities. Later, VII Corps completed clearing the Cotentin peninsula and captured Cherbourg, then played a major role in the breakout from Normandy during Operation 'Cobra'. In the autumn, Collins' 1st Infantry and 3rd Armored Divisions were largely instrumental in finally capturing Aachen on 21 October before moving up to the Rur river line in November.

When his 1st, and then 9th, Infantry Divisions went to V Corps over 17-19 December, Collins got the 78th back but this remained in the northern, Monschau, sector opposite elements of the German Sixth Panzer and Fifteenth Armies. His forces for the battle west of the Ourthe and during the subsequent counter-offensive were still amongst the strongest in Europe, with two 'heavy' armored divisions and two fresh infantry divisions at virtually full establishment. Collins faced the new challenge with, if not equanimity, at least confidence. And, when the time came to begin planning the Allied comeback to regain the initiative, it was Collins to whom Eisenhower, Bradley and Montgomery listened.

At a meeting with both Hodges and Patton at First Army headquarters on 27 December, which the SHAEF chief of staff, Lieutenant-General Walter

On 23 December, the day St Vith was evacuated, Lawton Collins was entrusted by Montgomery with the conduct of all operations west of the river Ourthe. (Eisenhower had given the field marshal command of the U.S. First and Ninth Armies on the 20th, leaving Omar Bradley with 'just' Patton's Third Army, which now included VIII Corps.)

Collins himself was one of the most experienced and audacious corps commanders in the Ardennes. Neither as methodical as Troy Middleton nor as impetuous as Leonard Gerow, he had won his

Bedell Smith, also attended, Collins proposed three alternative plans. By this time, Fifth Panzer Armee's drive to the Meuse had been permanently stopped at Celles, the northern and southern shoulders of the Allied line were secure, and only Bastogne remained under threat even though Patton's III Corps had broken the siege. The whole situation was entirely different to what it had been 10 days earlier. The Allies were no longer simply responding to German moves.

Two of Collins' plans aimed at a junction between III and VII Corps in the Bastogne region, while the third had St Vith as its objective. All, in Patton's view, were limited and he offered a much more ambitious proposal for major armoured thrusts by First and Third Armies from north and south to cut off the whole salient at the shoulders, trapping all German units still in the Ardennes. This, however, would have meant closing the jaws on an 80-mile (120-km) front along narrow roads in rugged terrain in the middle of winter, with adequate air support a constant question mark.

In the end the two Army commanders thrashed out a compromise using elements of all three of Collins' plans. VII Corps would initiate a First Army drive to link up with III and VIII Corps east of Houfalize, while XVIII (Airborne) Corps would attack from north and west towards St Vith. The plan was very similar in concept, in fact, to the 'small solution' proposed by the three German Armee commanders when they were first briefed about Operation 'Herbstnebel'. Unlike Hitler, however, Eisenhower accepted Collins' modified plan.

After the battle of Foy-Notre-Dame, an M3 of the 82nd Armored Reconnaissance Battalion, 2nd Armored Division, passes one of von Böhm's PzKpfw IVs, which appears undamaged, and may simply have run out of fuel. (U.S. Army)

Montgomery, of course, demurred, seeing an erosion of his authority. Although he was ready to consider counter-attack plans by the 27th (which elicited a spontaneous 'Praise God from whom all blessings flow!' from Eisenhower), he wanted to 'tidy up' the battlefield first, and bring more British reserves into play because he felt the Germans still had more cards up their sleeves. (British intelligence supported Montgomery's caution, but Eisenhower placed more reliance on 'Ultra' intercepts, which revealed the heavy German losses in men and armour.)

Reluctantly, then, Montgomery acceded to pressure, seeing his command of the U.S. First and Ninth Armies slipping from his grasp again, and a date was set: 3 January. Within 24 hours of the beginning of the counter-offensive there was no longer any threat to Bastogne. Four days later Hitler authorised Feldmarschall Walter Model to begin a limited withdrawal. And on 16 January patrols from Collins' 84th Infantry and Middleton's 11th Armored Division shook hands on the heights outside Houffalize. A few days later, XVIII Corps' troops recaptured St Vith. Collins' plan had worked, with VII Corps playing a leading role, and the enemy was in full retreat.

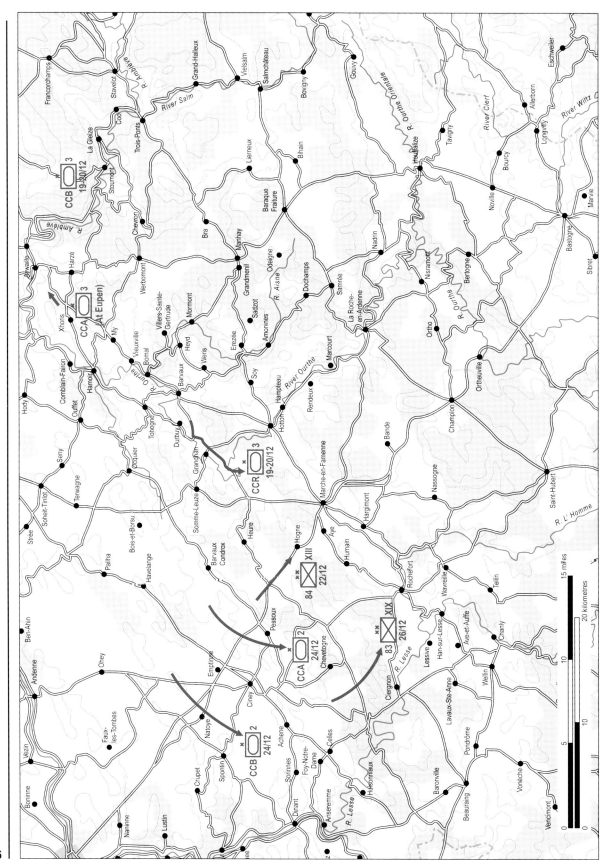

2nd Armored Division

'Hell on Wheels'

On 16 December 1944 Major-General Ernest Harmon's 2nd Armored Division was resting in Ninth Army reserve northeast of Maastricht, having reached the Rur river line on 28 November. The peace did not last long. As soon as Montgomery was given command of both Hodges' First and Simpson's Ninth Armies on 20 December, he began stripping the latter to reinforce the threatened sector in the Ardennes, and 2nd Armored moved to the

Major-General Ernest Harmon was highly experienced, having commanded 2nd Armored twice, once in Tunisia and now in the Ardennes. In between he was CO of 1st Armored in Italy. (U.S. Army)

> ### 2nd ARMORED DIVISION
> *Major-General Ernest M. Harmon*
> HQ Company and HQ Companies,
> Combat Commands A (Collier), B (White) & R (Hinds)
>
> ---
>
> 66 Armored Regiment (Collier)
> 67 Armored Regiment (White)
> 41 Armored Infantry Regiment (Hinds)
> 14 Armored Field Artillery Battalion (M7)
> 78 Armored Field Artillery Battalion (M7)
> 92 Armored Field Artillery Battalion (M7)
> 82 Armored Reconnaissance Battalion
> 17 Armored Engineer Battalion
> 48 Armored Medical Battalion
> 142 Armored Signal Company
> 2 Armored Maintenance Battalion
> 2 Armored Supply Battalion
> 502 Counter-Intelligence Corps Detachment
> 702 Tank Destroyer Battalion (M10/M36) (attached)
> 195 Anti-Aircraft Artillery Auto-Weapons Battalion (M15/M16)
>   (attached)

vicinity of Durbuy/Marche over the 22nd–23rd. This fortuitously put it in just the right place to inflict a singular defeat on its namesake, 2 Panzer Division.

Ninth Army's 2nd Armored Division, now reassigned to Collins' VII Corps, was one of the two strongest formations in northwest Europe. Both the 2nd and 3rd, alongside 1st Armored (which was in Italy), had escaped the army reorganisation of September 1943 and retained the old 'heavy' format of March 1942. This gave them each 232 medium and 158 light tanks in two armoured regiments compared with the 186 medium and 77 light in the three tank battalions of a 'triangular' light armoured division such as the 9th or 11th.

The 2nd Armored had been activated at Fort Benning, Georgia, on 15 July 1940 under Major-General Charles Scott; six months later he was

VII Corps was redeployed after Montgomery was given command of all Allied ground forces north of the 'Bulge' and Lawton Collins was entrusted with the conduct of all operations west of the river Ourthe. Later the corps advanced to Houffalize to link up with troops of Third Army advancing northward.

succeeded by none other than George S. Patton, Jr. Harmon assumed command in September 1944, taking over from Major-General Edward Brooks, who had led the division ashore in Normandy in June. In fact, Harmon felt quite at home in his new appointment because he had earlier commanded 2nd Armored during Operation 'Torch' in 1942.

Only part of the division was involved in this Anglo-American invasion of French northwest Africa which was designed to provide an 'anvil' on to which Montgomery`s Eighth Army could 'hammer' the Afrika Korps. The 66th Armored Regiment landed at Mehdia and the 67th at Fedala/Safi on 8 November. Three days later they took the surrender of Mazagan and subsequently fought in the Tunisian campaign, avoiding the fate of 1st Armored Division, which was severely mauled at Kasserine.

The division did not fight as a whole until the invasion of Sicily in July 1943, now commanded by Major-General Hugh Gaffey (who would lead 4th Armored Division to the relief of Bastogne in December 1944). Harmon himself, meanwhile, had taken over the 1st Armored Division, which he led successfully in Italy, playing a prominent role in saving the day at Anzio.

Back on Sicily, 2nd Armored Division`s Combat Command A landed at Licata and CCB east of Gela. On 15 July the two commands were reunited at Campobello and spearheaded the drive on Palermo. After the last German and Italian troops evacuated the island, 2nd Armored shipped to England to begin intensive training for D-Day.

Now commanded by Edward Brooks, who had led the 11th 'light' Armored Division from its formation until March this year, 2nd Armored was part of XIX Corps, which came ashore across 'Omaha' beach on 9 June, and advanced alongside the 30th Infantry Division through Isigny to the Taute river line south of Carentan. After helping to seal off the Cotentin peninsula and repulsing the German counter-attack towards Avranches on 7 August, the division captured Domfort and then advanced west of Dreux to help cut off those German forces still south of the river Seine between Paris and Elbeuf.

By the beginning of September the division was near Cambrai; a fortnight later it was across the Albert Canal and assaulted across the river Maas under heavy fire, with CCA at Valkenburg and CCB at Meerseen. The 2nd Armored consolidated its bridgehead and drove the Germans back to Sittard, but then faced a determined counter-attack, which forced the division into defensive positions near Geilenkirchen.

With German resistance intensifying now they were on their own soil, 2nd Armored fought several major battles over the next two months, with heavy losses

amongst its Shermans. Crossing the river Wurm at Marienburg on 3 October, CCB attacked from Übach next day and had to be reinforced by CCA, but was still stopped short of Geilenkirchen. There was further heavy fighting at Bäsweiler and Oidtweiler before the division started moving towards the Aachen Gap at Würselen in the middle of the month. A month later the division had taken Paffendorf and was pushing at the strong Jülich defences; again CCA had to reinforce CCB in the face of a counter-attack, but it took Apweiler and held it against determined efforts to throw them out.

Renewing its advance through heavy rain on 20 November, the division took Merzenhausen on the 27th after a five-day battle and reached the river Rur next day. It was now relieved in the line to recuperate and was in Ninth Army reserve when it was rushed south over 22–23 December, CCA reaching Buissonville on Christmas Eve and CCB inflicting a major defeat on 2 Panzer Division at Celles next day.

After clearing Humain, 2nd Armored was relieved by the 83rd Infantry Division on 28 December but took part in the counter-attack towards Houffalize beginning on 3 January 1945. After fighting its way through Odeigne, the division reached the river Ourthe and captured Houffalize on the 16th. Withdrawn to rest and make good its losses, the division was not in action again until 1 March, attacking across the Köln Plain to reach Verdingen on the Rhein three days later. It crossed on 27 March, relieved the 17th Airborne Division and attacked towards the Teutoburger Wald at the beginning of April. The division reached the river Elbe on 11 April, assaulted Magdeburg and finished mopping up before the official German surrender on 7 May 1945.

An M4 of 2nd Armored Division advances through a Christmas card landscape, but the ambulance travelling in the opposite direction testifies to the real brutality of the situation. (U.S. Signal Corps)

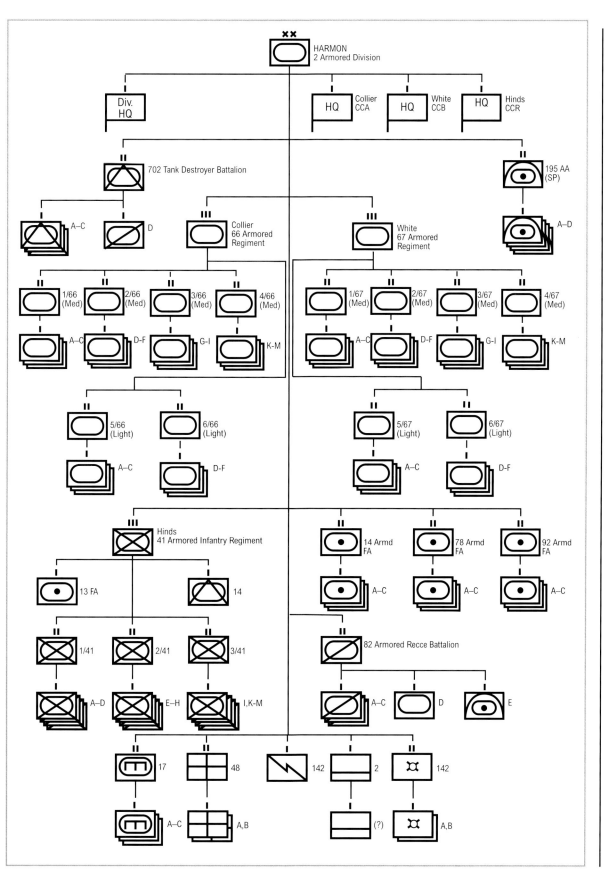

HARMON
2 Armored Division

Div. HQ

HQ Collier CCA

HQ White CCB

HQ Hinds CCR

702 Tank Destroyer Battalion

A–C

D

Collier 66 Armored Regiment

White 67 Armored Regiment

195 AA (SP)

A–D

1/66 (Med)

2/66 (Med)

3/66 (Med)

4/66 (Med)

1/67 (Med)

2/67 (Med)

3/67 (Med)

4/67 (Med)

A–C

D-F

G-I

K-M

A–C

D-F

G-I

K-M

5/66 (Light)

6/66 (Light)

5/67 (Light)

6/67 (Light)

A–C

D-F

A–C

D-F

Hinds 41 Armored Infantry Regiment

14 Armd FA

78 Armd FA

92 Armd FA

13 FA

14

A–C

A–C

A–C

1/41

2/41

3/41

82 Armored Recce Battalion

A–D

E–H

I,K-M

A–C

D

E

17

48

142

2

142

A–C

A,B

(?)

A,B

3rd Armored Division

'Spearhead'

While it was the 2nd Armored Division's privilege to demolish 2 Panzer Division almost on the bank of the river Meuse, it was 3rd Armored's prerogative to administer the coup de grâce to Kampfgruppe 'Peiper', the spearhead battlegroup of 1 SS-Panzer Division Leibstandarte 'Adolf Hitler', at La Gleize.

Rated by many soldiers and historians the best American tank commander of the war, Major-General Maurice Rose drove everywhere in an unarmoured Jeep, and the Ardennes in December 1944 were no exception. He arrived in the lines of the 82nd Airborne Division's 325th Glider Infantry Regiment near Werbomont shortly before midnight on 19 December while Brigadier-General Truman Boudinot's Combat Command B was only just beginning to assemble further north at Theux before its assault on Peiper.

After conferring with the commander of XVIII (Airborne) Corps, Matthew Ridgway, Rose drove on to Hotton, where he established his forward command post alongside that of Colonel Robert Howze`s CCR. (Unlike Combat Commands in the 'triangular'

Major-General Maurice Rose's skilful conduct of the counter-offensive in January 1945 was followed by his untimely death in action in March. He was succeeded by his CCA commander, Doyle Hickey. (U.S. Army)

divisions, which were more or less identical, CCR in the three 'heavy' divisions was ad hoc, and in 3rd Armored's case consisted of just the 83rd Reconnaissance Battalion, one battalion of infantry, one company of Shermans, two of M5s and a com-pany from the 23rd Engineer Battalion.)

Combat Command A, under Brigadier-General Doyle Hickey, had been deployed in defence of Eupen, where V Corps' commander, Leonard Gerow, had his headquarters. A few days later, when it became clear that Eupen was not threatened, CCA

3rd ARMORED DIVISION
Major-General Maurice Rose
HQ Company and HQ Companies,
Combat Commands A (Hickey), B (Boudinot) & R (Howze)

---

32 Armored Regiment (Hickey)
33 Armored Regiment (Boudinot)
36 Armored Infantry Regiment (Howze)
54 Armored Field Artillery Battalion (M7)
67 Armored Field Artillery Battalion (M7)
391 Armored Field Artillery Battalion (M7)
83 Armored Reconnaissance Battalion (Yeomans)
23 Armored Engineer Battalion
45 Armored Medical Battalion
143 Armored Signal Company
3 Armored Maintenance Battalion
3 Armored Supply Battalion
503 Counter-Intelligence Corps Detachment
643 Tank Destroyer Battalion (M18)
  (attached 22-26 December)
486 Anti-Aircraft Artillery Auto-Weapons Battalion (M15/M16)
  (attached)

---

was also brought south to help in the Allied counter-attack, which would begin on 3 January 1945.

The 3rd Armored Division was not as experienced as the 2nd but had already had an eventful war. Formed at Fort Beauregard, Louisiana, on 15 April 1941 under Major-General Alvin Gillem, it was not deployed in North Africa even though it had undergone rigorous desert training in California. Nor was it destined for Italy, but instead shipped to England in September 1943 to begin further training for the European theatre of operations.

Now commanded by Major-General Leroy Watson, the division landed in Normandy as part of VII Corps on 23 June 1944 and was immediately thrown into battle northeast of St Lô against the German salient at Villiers-Fossard, while the corps' infantry completed clearing the Cotentin peninsula and finally captured Cherbourg on the 27th.

Montgomery, still at this time in overall command of all Allied ground forces in France, wanted Bradley to pivot his First Army's left flank (V Corps) on Caumont and begin to drive north with his remaining three corps (VII, VIII and XIX) from the base of the Cotentin

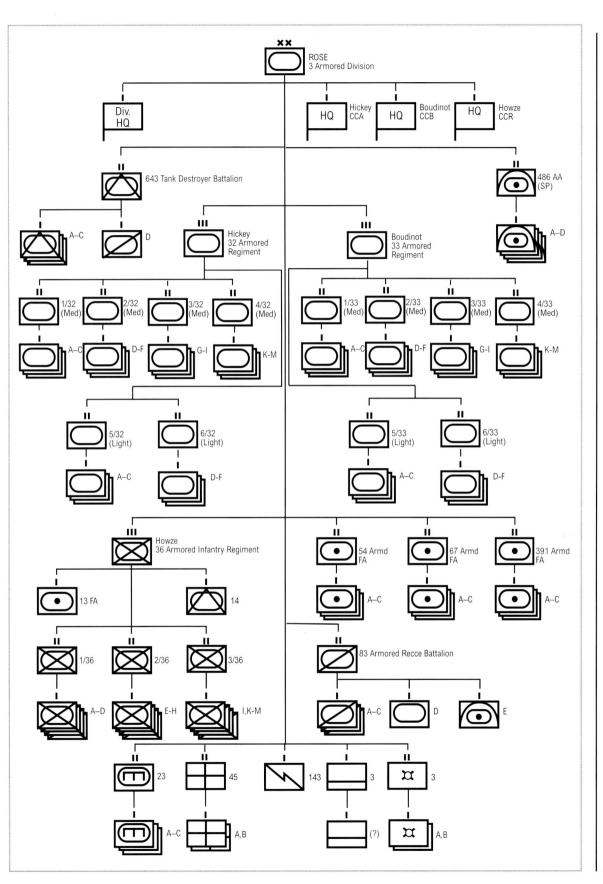

ROSE
3 Armored Division

Div. HQ

HQ — Hickey CCA

HQ — Boudinot CCB

HQ — Howze CCR

643 Tank Destroyer Battalion

486 AA (SP)

A–C

D

A–D

Hickey
32 Armored Regiment

Boudinot
33 Armored Regiment

1/32 (Med)

2/32 (Med)

3/32 (Med)

4/32 (Med)

1/33 (Med)

2/33 (Med)

3/33 (Med)

4/33 (Med)

A–C

D-F

G-I

K-M

A–C

D-F

G-I

K-M

5/32 (Light)

6/32 (Light)

5/33 (Light)

6/33 (Light)

A–C

D-F

A–C

D-F

Howze
36 Armored Infantry Regiment

54 Armd FA

67 Armd FA

391 Armd FA

13 FA

14

A–C

A–C

A–C

1/36

2/36

3/36

83 Armored Recce Battalion

A–D

E-H

I,K-M

A–C

D

E

23

45

143

3

3

A–C

A,B

(?)

A,B

M4s of 3rd Armored advancing towards Houffalize keep their turret machine-guns trained on the woods for enemy infantry armed with Panzerfausts. (U.S. Army)

peninsula across the Carentan Plain. On the right flank, Troy Middleton's VIII Corps would lead off on 3 July through La Haye du Puits towards Coutances; Collins' VII Corps would follow next day along the Carentan–Périers highway, while Charles Corlett's XIX Corps would advance on St Lô.

Not all of the attacks went anything like according to plan, largely as a result of the dense bocage countryside. Nevertheless, 3rd Armored reached the Hauts-Vents crossroads by 11 July, whereupon CCB captured Marigny and CCA fought its way across the river Sienne at the end of the month.

Early in August the division re-mustered and helped close the neck of the Falaise Pocket in which the Germans lost so many men and vehicles. Crossing the river Seine towards the end of the month, 3rd Armored pursued a disintegrating enemy over the rivers Marne and Aisne to capture the little town of Huy on the Meuse on 6 September. The division helped clear Liège, overran the defenders at Verviers, and arrived at the Siegfried Line (West Wall) at Schmidthof on 12 September.

Pressing into Germany towards Aachen, which would be the first major German city to fall into Allied hands, CCB broached the formidable West Wall's concrete and steel barriers near Rötgen on 13 September while CCA pushed through similar obstacles to reach Nutheim and Eilendorf. Over the next few days the division was stalled at Geisbach and Mausbach and could not take Stolberg until the 22nd,

but was then thrown out of Donnerburg.

During most of October and early November the division was heavily involved in the battle around Aachen, taking heavy losses from minefields as well as accurate and determined enemy fire. When the city finally fell, 3rd Armored pushed on rapidly to the river Rur and captured Geich on 11 December. There was still no respite because the division, its elements widely separated, was hastily called south to help deal with the German Ardennes offensive.

After the battles at Stoumont/La Gleize, Hotton, Manhay/Grandmenil and Sadzot, the division attacked towards Houffalize to reunite First and Third Armies. Its men reached the river Ourthe on 19 January 1945 and captured Gouvy and Beho on the 22nd. The 'Battle of the Bulge' was, to all intents and purposes, over by this time, and a month later the division had secured two bridgeheads over the river Erft at Glesch and Paffendorf.

Shrugging off determined counter-attacks, 3rd Armored took the battle back to the enemy and, with the help of substantial air support, captured Stomeln on 3 March. Next day the weary troops could look down on the Rhein. The city of Köln fell after a two-day battle in which the 3rd Armored was greatly assisted by the 104th Infantry Division, which had newly joined VII Corps.

Crossing the Rhein on 23 March the division reached Marburg on the river Lahn five days later and, seething with fury at their popular commander's death in action, helped seal off the Ruhr pocket with victory at Paderborn on 1 April. CCA commander Doyle Hickey led the division across the rivers Weser and Mulde to Dessau before the end of hostilities.

83rd Infantry Division
'Thunderbolt'

Although actually part of VIII Corps at the beginning of the German offensive on 16 December 1944, Robert Macon's division played its decisive part in the 'battle of the bulge' after it was reassigned to VII Corps on the 26th. Prior to that it contained a German attack towards Guerzenich on the 16th, relieved the 5th Infantry Division (XIX Corps) on the 22nd and fought a major battle for Winden over Christmas before being transferred to VII Corps and moved to the Havelange area, where it relieved 2nd Armored Division. Heavy fighting followed at Rochefort and in January at Langlir and Bovigny before the division was pulled back to Holland for rehabilitation at the end of the month.

The 83rd had been activated at Camp Atterbury, Indiana, on 15 August 1942, commanded by Major-General Frank Milburn. Robert Macon took over in January 1944 and shipped his division to England in April. It landed in Normandy across 'Omaha' beach on 19 June and took part in the VIII Corps' attack across the Carentan Plain towards Périers on 4 July.

After regrouping, the division took part in the 'Cobra' breakout on the 26th, crossed the river Taute and followed 6th Armored Division into Brittany, reaching the heavily fortified port of St Malo on 4 August. The determined German commander evacuated the French civilian population before the siege began in earnest, and it was a bitter struggle for strongpoint after strongpoint. The last, The Citadel, did not fall until 17 August after the defenders were warned that they were going to be bombed with napalm.

While the bulk of the division now left Brittany and moved south to the river Loire west of Orléans on 27 August, a rearguard remained behind and made an amphibious assault on the Ile de Cézembre, off St Malo, on 2 September. Reunited, the division patrolled the banks of the Loire south of Rennes until it was reassigned to XX Corps and moved east to the river Mosel at Remich on the 25th. There was further heavy fighting as the 83rd crossed the Sauer and advanced towards the West Wall, with the 329th Regiment involved in a pitched battle at Grevenmacher at the beginning of October before capturing Echternach.

Transferred back to VIII Corps, the division took Le Stromberg hill at Basse Knoz on 5 November and held it against counter-attack, then relieved the

---

83rd INFANTRY DIVISION
Major-General Robert C. Macon
HQ Company

329 Infantry Regiment
330 Infantry Regiment
331 Infantry Regiment
322 Field Artillery Battalion (105mm)
323 Field Artillery Battalion (105mm)
324 Field Artillery Battalion (155mm)
908 Field Artillery Battalion (105mm)
83 Reconnaissance Troop, Mechanized
308 Engineer Combat Battalion
308 Medical Battalion
83 Signal Company
83 Quartermaster Company
783 Ordnance Light Maintenance Company
Military Police Platoon
453 Anti-Aircraft Artillery Auto-Weapons Battalion (40mm)
  (attached)
774 Tank Battalion (detached 24 December)
629 Tank Destroyer Battalion (M10) (Anderson)
  (detached 23 December)
772 Tank Destroyer Battalion (towed)
  (attached 22 December)

4th Infantry Division west of the river Rur and captured Strass and Gey on 10 December. Four days later it contained a further counter-attack towards Guerzenich before being briefly assigned to XIX Corps for the attack on Winden over 23–25 December.

After fighting in the Ardennes with VII Corps from 26 December, the division moved to a rest area at the end of January before rejoining XIX Corps on 16 February for the remainder of the war. It took part in Operation 'Grenade', crossing the river Erft before reaching the Rhein at Oberkassel on 3 March.

Crossing the river south of Wesel on the 29th and driving across the Münster Plain, the division established a bridgehead over the Lippe at Hamm at the beginning of April, captured Neuhaus, crossed the Weser and overran Halle. Pushing on into the Harz Mountains, the 83rd reached the river Elbe on 12 April. Repulsing counter-attacks, the division made contact with Red Army troops on the 28th and finished mopping up around Zerbst.

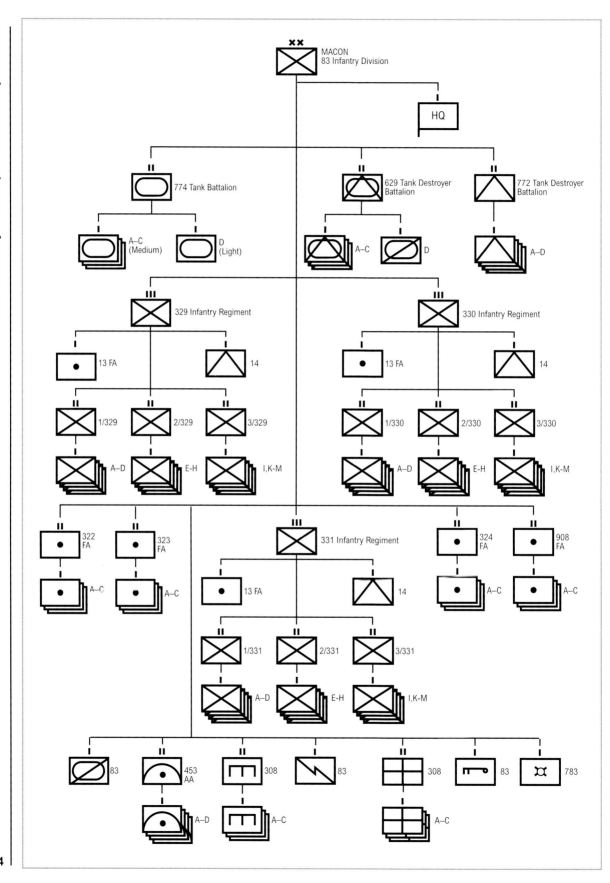

84th Infantry Division

'Railsplitters'

The 84th was transferred from XIII to VII Corps on 21 December 1944 and moved to the vicinity of Marche, where it established a perimeter defence. Although its lines were pierced between Marche and Hotton during a fierce battle in sleet and snow on the 23rd, the division recaptured Verdenne on Christmas Day and repulsed attacks towards Ménil. On 3 January it followed 2nd Armored Division towards Houffalize as part of the counter-offensive to reunite First and Third Armies and restore control of the former to Bradley, who, along with Eisenhower, had been chafing at Montgomery's indecision. The division recaptured the Baraque Fraiture crossroads southeast of Manhay and captured Laroche on 11 January. After a brief respite, the 84th then retook Gouvy, Beho and Ortheuville over the 22nd-23rd.

The 84th had been formed at Camp Howze, Texas, on 15 October 1942 under Major-General John Hildring. Its next CO in February 1943 was Major-General Stonewall Jackson, and there were two other changes in command before Alexander Bolling took over in June 1944. The division sailed to England in September and landed in France across 'Omaha' beach on 1 November. Temporarily attached to the British XXX Corps at Gulpen in Holland, the division fought in the Würselen area before, now with the U.S. XIII Corps, attacking towards Geilenkirchen to reduce the salient north of Aachen.

Supported by British flail tanks, the division began its attack on 18 November and captured Prummern two days later. The 334th Regiment captured Mahogany Hill on the 22nd but the 333rd lost heavily in its own attack on Müllendorf the same day, and on the 23rd the attack was called off when all attempts to take Wurm and Beeck failed. These were shortlived setbacks. Launching a surprise assault without the usual prior artillery bombardment to alert the enemy, the 335th Regiment finally took Beeck on 30 November.

At the beginning of December the 84th began driving towards the river Rur but, on the day the German Ardennes offensive started, the 16th, the division's lines were pierced at Leifarth. Rallying rapidly, the 84th responded aggressively and finally took Wurm two days later.

Reassigned to VII Corps, the division took its place

84th INFANTRY DIVISION
Brigadier-General Alexander R. Bolling
HQ Company

---

333 Infantry Regiment (Pedley)
334 Infantry Regiment (Hoy)
335 Infantry Regiment (Parker)
325 Field Artillery Battalion (105mm)
326 Field Artillery Battalion (105mm)
327 Field Artillery Battalion (155mm)
84 Reconnaissance Troop, Mechanized
309 Engineer Combat Battalion
309 Medical Battalion
84 Signal Company
84 Quartermaster Company
784 Ordnance Light Maintenance Company
Military Police Platoon
557 Anti-Aircraft Artillery Auto-Weapons Battalion (40mm) (attached)
701 Tank Battalion (detached 20 December)
771 Tank Battalion (attached 20 December)
638 Tank Destroyer Battalion (M18) (attached)

---

in the line on the flank of XVIII (Airborne) Division, at the time only lightly held by elements of 3rd Armored Division. It harassed the flank of 2 Panzer Division as the German column headed towards Dinant and, in conjunction with CCA of 2nd Armored Division, was involved in heavy fighting around Rochefort.

After the conclusion of the 'Battle of the Bulge', the 84th relieved the 102nd Infantry Division, XIII Corps, on 7 February 1945 and assaulted across the Rur at Linnich on the 23rd. After capturing Krefeld in a two-day battle over 2–3 March, the division reached the Rhein on the 5th. After very nearly capturing bridges at Rheinhausen and Homberg, the 84th went on to the defensive and did not get across the river until 1 April.

Moving swiftly up to the Weser, the division established a bridgehead south of Neesen, then over the Leine near Gümmer. Hannover fell on 10 April and the 84th relieved the 5th Armored Division on the Elbe on the 16th. After mopping up the sector, the division made contact with advancing Red Army troops near Below on 2 May and finished the war on occupation duties.

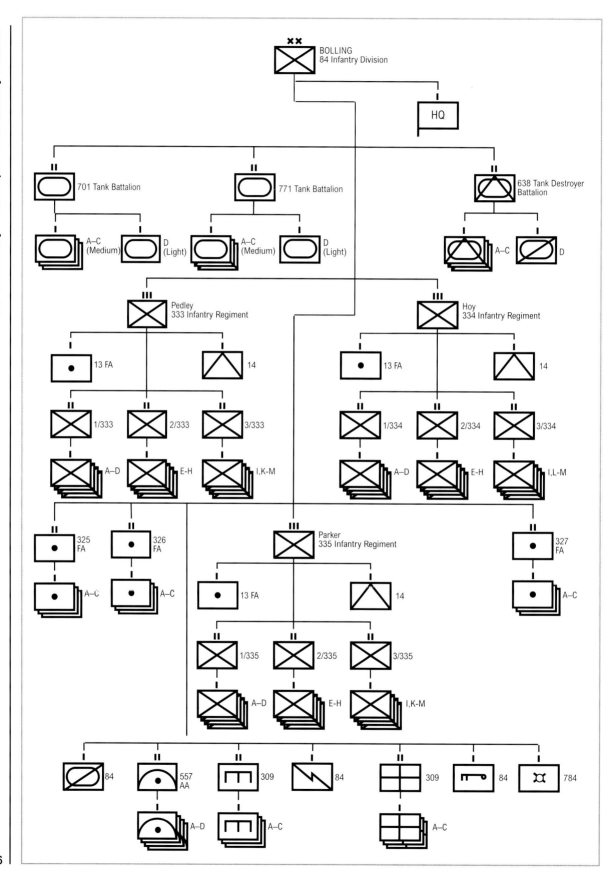

U.S. VII CORPS' BATTLES

CCB, 3rd Armored Division

Stoumont/La Gleize – December 20–25

Kampfgruppe 'Peiper', the spearhead not just of 1 SS-Panzer Division Leibstandarte 'Adolf Hitler' but also of the whole of Sixth Panzer Armee, had become something of a 'bogeyman' to the Allies as Christmas approached. After the massacre of American prisoners near Malmédy, it was no longer a matter of stopping the battlegroup's westward advance; it had to be exterminated. The result, for Brigadier-General Raymond Boudinot's CCB of 3rd Armored Division, was a difficult battle since both the terrain and interior lines of communication were in the enemy's favour.

Peiper's force had managed to get as far as Stoumont by 19 December but was prevented from getting any further by the 119th Regiment of 30th Infantry Division. By this time the Kampfgruppe was so low on fuel, as well as ammunition and food, that Peiper had abandoned all thought of any further advance anyway. The town of Stavelot to his east was securely in American hands despite attempts to dislodge it by the Leibstandarte's Kampfgruppen

'Knittel' and 'Sandig'. This meant that no further supplies could get through to Peiper from the east, and the only hope of salvation lay with the division's fourth battlegroup, Kampfgruppe 'Hansen', which reached the heights between Wanne and Trois Ponts during the night of 20–21 December.

Trois Ponts by now was occupied by a battalion of the 82nd Airborne, while other paras were hacking at Peiper's rearguard at Cheneux. With a breakthrough no longer possible, Peiper was forced to withdraw the bulk of his battlegroup to the hills and woods surrounding La Gleize. On the way, however, he had captured an interesting prisoner.

Earlier, acting on instructions to delay Kampfgruppe 'Peiper' long enough to allow the 82nd Airborne Division time to deploy, Major Hal McCown's II/119th had established a blocking position between Werbomont and Trois Ponts. When the paras of II/505th PIR relieved them, McCown led his men back north to rejoin their regiment. On a reconnaissance on 21 December, he became perhaps the most

3rd Armored Division M4s with 105mm guns – a modified version of the standard field piece – fire either by radio direction or from map grid references over a wooded hill. American artillery was a decisive factor throughout the campaign. (U.S. Army)

16/12/1944	17/12	18/12	19/12	20/12	21/12	22/12	23/12	24/12	25/12	26/12	27/12	28/12	29/12
pages 66-72	77-78	73-76	79-82,85-86	31-34,83-84	87-88,94-95	39-40	35-38,89-90						

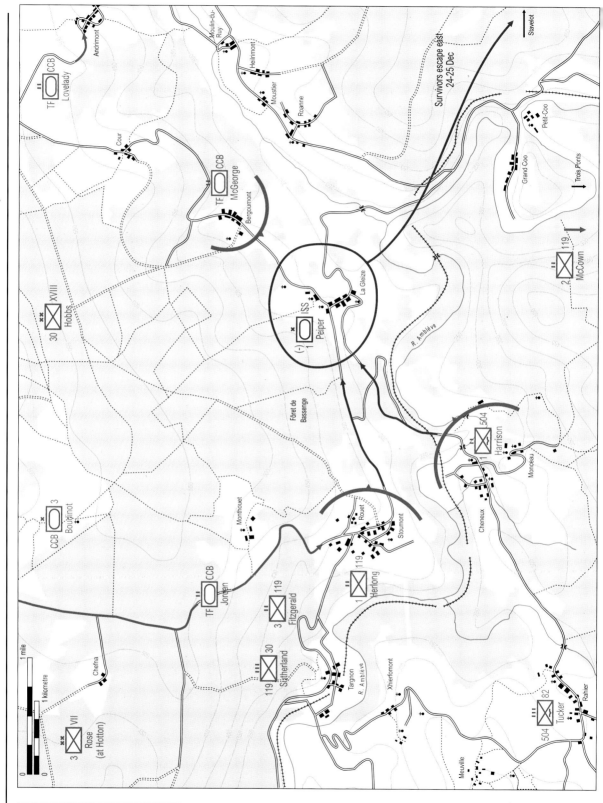

16/12/1944	17/12	18/12	19/12	20/12	21/12	22/12	23/12	24/12	25/12	26/12	27/12	28/12	29/12
pages 66-72	77-78	73-76	79-82,85-86	31-34,83-84	87-88,94-95	39-40		35-38,89-90					

The spoils of victory: GIs labour to refuel one of Peiper's abandoned Tiger IIs on a farm just outside La Gleize. (U.S. Army)

celebrated prisoner of the battle, and even later featured in *Stars & Stripes*.

That evening Peiper – who spoke good English – talked with him over a cup of coffee in the flickering candlelight of his command post. McCown later said that although he found Peiper's fanaticism to the Nazi cause difficult to understand, he gradually came to admire him, and believed his assurance that the other American prisoners he had – many of them wounded – would be treated well. By this time the village of La Gleize was being gradually pounded to rubble by U.S. field artillery and the conversation went on all night because it was impossible to sleep.

Boudinot's combat command had arrived at Theux, just to the northwest of Spa and about 10 miles (16 km) directly north of Stoumont, during the morning of the previous day, 20 December. Sizing up the situation, which was pretty clear-cut, Boudinot promptly split CCB into three task forces. The smallest, under Captain John Jordan, headed directly south from Theux and attempted to help I/119th Infantry's attack towards Stoumont. Jordan's tanks came under enfilading fire from hull-down Panzers and the two leading Shermans were knocked out, blocking the road. By this time it was almost dark, and there was nothing more to be done until the morning.

While Task Force 'Jordan' helped recapture Stoumont on 22 December, and Task Force 'Lovelady' cut off Peiper's eastward escape route, Task Force 'McGeorge' bottled off the northern exit from La Gleize.

The largest task force, under Lieutenant-Colonel William Lovelady, was given the most easterly assignment of cutting the road between Stavelot and La Gleize, splitting Kampfgruppe 'Peiper' off from the remaining elements of Kampfgruppe 'Knittel' still trying to retake Stavelot from the west. In so doing, Lovelady ran into elements of Kampfgruppe 'Hansen' heading northwest from Wanne to help Peiper. The German column was shot up and Lovelady established roadblocks to complete sealing Peiper in from all but his last possible escape route southeast.

Boudinot's third battlegroup, commanded by Major Kenneth McGeorge, headed almost due south from Spa, in the middle of the other two CCB task forces, and reached the outskirts of La Gleize before it was thrown back and forced to retire for the night to the hamlet of Bourgoumont.

The shortest day of the year, 21 December, was a sparring match. Peiper's tanks and assault guns, unable to move because of lack of fuel, were well dug-in with plenty of infantry armed with Panzerfausts to deter any American tanks that ventured too close. Boudinot could not deploy his Shermans effectively anyway because the terrain restricted them to the narrow, sunken roads.

On 22 December Stoumont was finally recaptured. Peiper had withdrawn everything into the La Gleize

16/12/1944	17/12	18/12	19/12	20/12	21/12	22/12	23/12	24/12	25/12	26/12	27/12	28/12	29/12
pages 66-72	77-78	73-76	79-82,85-86	31-34,83-84	87-88,94-95	39-40		35-38,89-90					

enclave, leaving behind just those wounded unable to walk. Task Force Lovelady had a fierce, predominantly infantry, skirmish west of Stavelot, and Task Force McGeorge beat back a reconnaissance sortie north of La Gleize. Meanwhile, the artillery, which had not ceased firing all night, continued to pound the village into rubble. Then, at about 2000 hrs, in response to Peiper's pleas for fuel, food and ammunition, 20 Luftwaffe Ju 52s attempted to drop him some supplies. Almost all fell into American hands in Stoumont.

By the 23rd Peiper knew for a certainty that his mission had failed, but all his requests to be allowed to try to fight his way out southeast fell on stony ground. The top German commanders were buoyed up by the excellent progress being made by Fifth Panzer Armee's spearheads and were convinced that if Peiper could just hold out for a couple of days, his problems would remove themselves.

As a day of battle, the 23rd was inconclusive. The shelling continued, with most of Peiper's infantry huddling in cellars, while the infantry of 3rd Armored and 30th Infantry Divisions tightened the noose around them, hampered by minefields and dug-in tanks and assault guns. CCB's tanks could not move effectively and, in light of more critical battles developing further south around Hotton, Boudinot was forced to withdraw some of his strength.

The end, when it came, came quickly, and Hal McCown re-enters the story. Peiper had finally, at about 1700 hrs, obtained permission from his Korps commander to evacuate La Gleize. With no fuel, he knew he had to abandon his tanks, and left a small rearguard behind to destroy them, as well as a detachment with the German wounded and American prisoners. McCown, warning Peiper that his agreement could not be binding on his superiors, signed a paper saying that, in return for Peiper releasing the Americans, the United States would return the German wounded when they had recovered. As surety, McCown gave his parole and accompanied the remaining survivors of the Kampfgruppe as they stole into the night at about 0200 hrs on Christmas Eve.

After hiding out in the woods during daylight, Peiper's men resumed their eastward trudge after dark. At some point, they brushed against a column of 82nd Airborne paras marching in the opposite direction. During the brief firefight, McCown threw himself flat and escaped when Peiper's men moved on, the 770 survivors of the original 5,000 reaching the Kampfgruppe 'Hansen' lines at about 1000 hrs on Christmas Day.

Meanwhile, their quarry having flown, the 'mudfeet' of 3rd Armored and 30th Infantry Divisions had an anti-climactic Christmas Eve. Though expecting heavy opposition, they were able to walk into La Gleize, capture about 300 Germans, mostly wounded, and congratulate the 170 prisoners freed by Peiper on their escape. Needless to say, the German prisoners were not repatriated! However, although denied a true battlefield victory, Boudinot's CCB could count, in the village of La Gleize itself, 28 tanks, 70 half-tracks and 25 guns, not to mention those littering the surrounding countryside. Kampfgruppe 'Peiper' had, indeed, been 'exterminated'.

Peiper was forced to abandon more than 90 vehicles when he evacuated his surviving men from the La Gleize pocket, including a large number of half-tracks (not shown) just to the southwest.

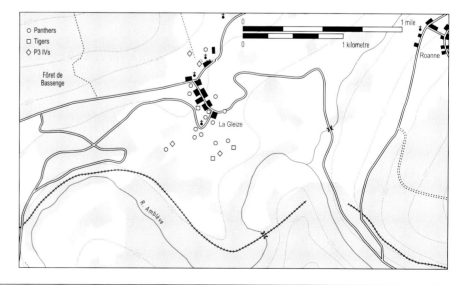

	16/12/1944	17/12	18/12	19/12	20/12	21/12	22/12	23/12	24/12	25/12	26/12	27/12	28/12	29/12
pages	66-72	77-78	73-76	79-82,85-86	31-34,83-84	87-88,94-95	39-40		35-38,89-90					

U.S. VII CORPS' BATTLES

CCR, 3rd Armored Division

Hotton – December 20–26

At about the same time on 20 December that Brigadier-General Raymond Boudinot was organising CCB for its assault on Kampfgruppe 'Peiper', the commander of 3rd Armored, Major-General Maurice Rose, arrived in the vicinity of Hotton. Since CCA was still at Eupen, all that Rose had at his disposal was Colonel Robert Howze's CCR with its command post at Soy, and Lieutenant-Colonel Prentice Yeomans' 83rd Armored Reconnaissance Battalion. At this point the incomplete division temporarily fell under XVIII (Airborne) Corps' command, on the right flank of 82nd Airborne Division. Ridgway asked Rose to reconnoitre towards the main Liège-Bastogne road (N15) and try to re-

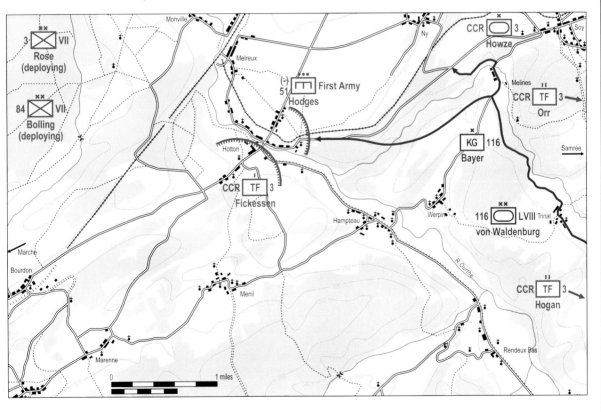

The defence of Hotton and the bridge over the Ourthe depended on a scratch force under Major Jack Fikessen while CCR/3rd Armored's small task forces sallied out to give battle to 116 Panzer Division.

establish contact with VIII Corps.

With the very limited strength at his disposal, Rose split his command into three task forces plus a reserve, knowing full well he was running a risk

16/12/1944	17/12	18/12	19/12	20/12	21/12	22/12	23/12	24/12	25/12	26/12	27/12	28/12	29/12
pages 66-72	77-78	73-76	79-82,85-86	27-30,33-34,83-84	87-88,94-95	39-40		35-38,89-90					

because any one of them could be wiped out if it ran into a strong Panzer formation. But he knew the old maxim that 'reconnaissance is never wasted'. Each of the task forces comprised a mechanised reconnaissance troop with M8s, a company of M4s, a platoon of M5s and a battery of M7s. In reserve, between Hotton and Soy, Howze retained one infantry battalion, the remaining company of M4s, two companies of M5s and two companies of engineers. In the north, the task force under Lieutenant-Colonel Matthew Kane headed towards Manhay and Malempré. In the centre, that under Major John Tucker headed through Dochamps towards Samrée, with the intention of then veering northeast towards Baraque Fraiture. In the south the force under Lieutenant-Colonel Sam Hogan headed for La Roche.

Task Force 'Tucker' ran into immediate problems because Samrée was already in the hands of the leading Kampfgruppe from 116 Panzer Division. After losing six Shermans, he fell back behind Dochamps. Rose promptly organised a fourth task force, comprising two companies of armoured infantry from Howze's reserve under Lieutenant-Colonel William Orr, and sent them off to assist Tucker in retaking Samrée. During the night of 20/21 December, however, the CO of 116 Panzer Division, Generalmajor Siegfried von Waldenburg, stole a march on Rose by sending his leading Kampfgruppe along a minor road through the hamlet of Beffe, smack in between Task Forces 'Hogan' and 'Tucker/Orr'. This debouched on to the main road between Soy and Hotton. Rose, at his command post in Erezée, heard the news at 0850 hrs, by which time the German attack on Hotton had already begun.

Apart from Task Force 'Kane' east of Manhay, which was unaffected by these events but which had 2 SS-Panzer Division bearing down on it, the others were forced to fall back, 'Tucker' and 'Orr' to Amonines and 'Hogan' to a wooded hill east of Marcouray. Hotton and its bridge over the Ourthe were only defended by a couple of hundred headquarters clerks, a few engineers and two M4s. The Shermans were destroyed almost immediately and one platoon of engineers was overrun, but three German tanks succumbed to bazookas and, amazingly, the remainder of the tiny garrison held on throughout the day.

The German commander did not know how weak the American forces opposing him were, he saw American tanks on just about every hill around and

After he rejected a German surrender demand, the USAAF attempted unsuccessfully to resupply Sam Hogan's task force, and he followed his men back through the woods to safety. (U.S. Signal Corps)

believed he was in a cul-de-sac. LVIII Korps' commander Walter Krüger concurred so, incredibly, while the bridge at Hotton was within his grasp, von Waldenburg pulled back his leading Kampfgruppe and sent it through La Roche towards Marche instead. 560 Volksgrenadier Division smoothly filled the gap during the night of 22/23 December.

Task Force 'Orr' attempted to retake Dochamps but was rebuffed with the loss of six M4s, and a flanking attack by 'Kane' was also unsuccessful because the tanks could not manoeuvre off the road as a result of the marshy ground. The fact that 3rd Armored was being reinforced now that it was again part of VII Corps had little immediate effect, because Brigadier-General Doyle Hickey's CCA, when it arrived from Eupen, had to be split to counter the threat from 2 SS-Panzer Division near Manhay, and throw out a screen towards St Hubert in the south. All that Rose received to reinforce Howze's CCR was one battalion of M4s and a company of infantry under Lieutenant-Colonel Walter Richardson. There was other help, though: the 509th and I/517th Parachute Infantry Battalions and the 188th Field Artillery Battery with a dozen 155mm guns from Corps reserve.

It was not enough to resume any offensive action for the time being, other than to force 560 Volksgrenadier Division to vacate the heights overlooking Hotton. Task Force 'Hogan', trapped in the woods outside Marcouray, had to spike its guns and tanks and retire to friendly lines on foot during Christmas night. Task Force 'Orr', even with Richardson's reinforcement, could not yet retake Dochamps or Samrée, and even though 560 Volksgrenadier Division was not making any overtly hostile moves, the threat posed by 2 SS-Panzer Division in the north and 2, 9, 116 and 130 Panzer Divisions to the south precluded more than hanging on with clenched teeth.

16/12/1944	17/12	18/12	19/12	20/12	21/12	22/12	23/12	24/12	25/12	26/12	27/12	28/12	29/12
pages 66-72	77-78	73-76	79-82,85-86	27-30,33-34,83-84	87-88,94-95	39-40		35-38,89-90					

U.S. VII CORPS' BATTLES

333rd and 334th Infantry Regiments

Marche/Verdenne – December 20–27

Leading elements of Brigadier-General Alexander Bolling's 84th Infantry Division began arriving in Marche a couple of hours before midnight on 20 December, and their commander himself next morning. About midday he sent a couple of platoons from Lieutenant-Colonel Charles Hoy's 334th Regiment to ascertain the situation in Hotton, and when they reported that the town and its bridge over the Ourthe were apparently safe for the time being, Bolling asked for orders. His assigned task was to screen the assembly area for VII Corps to the west but he was now told to hold on the Hotton-Marche line. As the rest of the division, plus the attached 771st Tank Battalion, arrived over the 21st-22nd, Bolling deployed them along a 12-mile (19-km) front with the 334th on his left, anchored on Hotton, and Colonel Hugh Parker's 335th in front of Marche itself. Colonel Timothy Pedley's 333rd was kept in reserve around Baillonville.

What First Army commander Courtney Hodges, and Ridgway and Collins, urgently needed was information about German movements south and west of the VII Corps' deployment area. During the 23rd, Bolling sent out patrols and put a rifle company into Rochefort. Later, on Corps orders, he extended his perimeter bastions by sending I/333rd far southwest to Wanlin, and III/335th to Rochefort.

By this time, 116 Panzer Division had disengaged at Hotton and, re-routed through La Roche, was approaching Marche. The commander of Fifth Panzer Armee, General von Manteuffel (who was driving right up front with Panzer Lehr), was concerned about the threat to his flank posed by the 84th Infantry. Accordingly, leaving Lehr to take Rochefort, he drove personally to order 116 Panzer's commander, von Waldenburg, to attack and cut the road north of Marche so as to interdict American reinforcements.

Bolling, who at this time was under the temporary

The ground was frozen so hard in places that the infantry could only dig shallow foxholes. The men of the 334th Regiment deployed between Hotton and Verdenne, where the 116 Panzer Division attack took place, could only be thankful that the German artillery was low on ammunition.
(U.S. Army)

16/12/1944	17/12	18/12	19/12	20/12	21/12	22/12	23/12	24/12	25/12	26/12	27/12	28/12	29/12
pages 66-72	77-78	73-76	79-82,85-86	27-32,83-84	87-88,94-95	39-40		35-38,89-90					

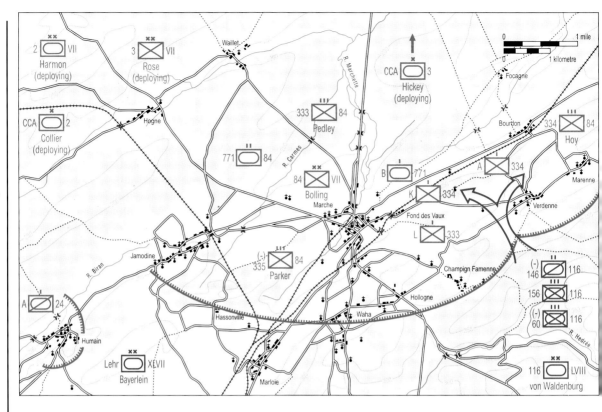

Although grenadiers of 116 Panzer Division got to within sight of the Hotton-Marche highway north of Verdenne, they were pinned down by Bolling's infantry and artillery and could make no further headway.

command of Ridgway's XVIII (Airborne) Corps while Collins was deploying 2nd Armored and CCA of 3rd Armored Division to his south and west, knew that a strong German armoured force was approaching up the west bank of the Ourthe from La Roche (which the 7th Armored Division trains had just escaped from), and extended his perimeter well forward of the vital Hotton–Marche road, which had now become the German LVIII Panzer Korps' objective.

Von Waldenburg began his attack by infiltrating two rifle companies through the woods towards Verdenne, at the junction of the 84th Infantry Division's 334th and 335th Regiments. However, the German troop movements had been spotted and at about midday on Christmas Eve Bolling sent I/334th, supported by M4s from the 771st Tank Battalion, to drive the intruders out. The victory was shortlived because, an hour later, von Waldenburg launched another force of grenadiers, supported by tanks, against Verdenne.

The village fell after bitter house-to-house fighting and von Waldenburg brought up artillery to help extend the wedge in 84th Infantry's lines.

Bolling counter-attacked at midnight with two companies of the 334th and one of the 333rd. One company of the 334th blundered into half a dozen German tanks and was decimated by high explosive and machine-gun fire, but the others pressed on and by dawn had cleared Verdenne, taking 289 prisoners. This, though, was not the end, for at noon on Christmas Day von Waldenburg sent in a company of nine tanks from 16 Panzer Regiment. Company B of the 771st Tank Battalion accounted for all of them. Then, on the next day, Bolling launched two fresh companies from the 333rd into the saucer-like depression which had become the battlefield. They were beaten back by I/60 Panzergrenadier Regiment, so for the remainder of the day Bolling contented himself by pounding the German positions with artillery fire. During the night, however, von Waldenburg pulled his troops out because they were more urgently needed elsewhere following the defeat of 2 Panzer Division at Celles, and the 84th Infantry patrols found deserted foxholes on the 27th.

16/12/1944	17/12	18/12	19/12	20/12	21/12	22/12	23/12	24/12	25/12	26/12	27/12	28/12	29/12
pages 66-72	77-78	73-76	79-82,85-86	27-32,83-84	87-88,94-95	39-40		35-38,89-90					

U.S. VII CORPS' BATTLES

CCB, 2nd Armored Division

Foy-Notre-Dame/Celles – December 24–26

Moved south in great secrecy from its rest area east of Maastricht, with orders to maintain strict radio silence, Major-General Ernest Harmon's 'Hell On Wheels' division completed its 70-mile (110-km) march from Ninth Army reserve to the vicinity of Durbuy, north of Marche, on 23 December. The move had been accomplished with only minor mishaps as a result of the slippery roads, and the division officially became part of the reconstituted VII Corps. At 1630 hrs the same day the corps officially assumed responsibility for the 50-mile (80-km) sector of front from the right flank of XVIII (Airborne) Corps, on the river Ourthe in the north, to Givet, on the Meuse, in the south.

The original plan was that the 2nd Armored was to spearhead a major counter-attack against the leading columns of Fifth Panzer Armee on 24 December, but events dictated otherwise. At lunchtime on the 23rd, while Harmon was conferring with his regimental officers, a report came in that an armoured car had been shot up near Ciney. Harmon decisively despatched Brigadier-General John Collier's Combat Command A towards this important junction with its main roads pointing straight towards Dinant and Namur, telling Lawton Collins what he had done afterwards. (The incident turned out to have been an accidental brush with a British patrol.)

Heading towards Buissonville and Rochefort, the leading battalions of Collier's 66th Armored Regiment and 41st Armored Infantry Regiment ran into a road-block in the village of Leignon set up by Kampfgruppe

'von Böhm', the reinforced reconnaissance battalion which was leading 2 Panzer Division's advance towards the Meuse. And, as more and more reports began to come in of German armour west of Marche, Harmon began deploying the rest of his division to the south and west of Brigadier-General Alexander Bolling's 84th Infantry Division.

On 24 December CCA became involved in a skirmish with the Panzer 'Lehr' Division near Rochefort; this division was forming the left flank support for 2 Panzer Division's advance and, as a result of the encounter with CCA, was unable to give that support. This had a significant effect on CCB's own battle further west over the next two days, as did CCA's capture of Buissonville and Humain, also on the 24th. This isolated the main body of 2 Panzer Division from its two leading Kampfgruppen, 'von Böhm' and the reinforced 304 Panzergrenadier Regiment 'von Cochenhausen'. These had reached Foy-Notre-Dame and the area Celles–Conneux late on the 23rd with the Meuse just a proverbial stone's throw away.

All through Christmas Eve Harmon had been getting reports of a strong concentration of German

The bridge too far for 2 Panzer Division was the one at Dinant. If 2nd Armored Division and the British 29th Armoured Brigade had not stopped it just short of here, Bruxelles was just down the road.
(Imperial War Museum)

16/12/1944	17/12	18/12	19/12	20/12	21/12	22/12	23/12	24/12	25/12	26/12	27/12	28/12	29/12
pages 66-72	77-78	73-76	79-82,85-86	27-34,83-84	87-88,94-95	39-40		89-90					

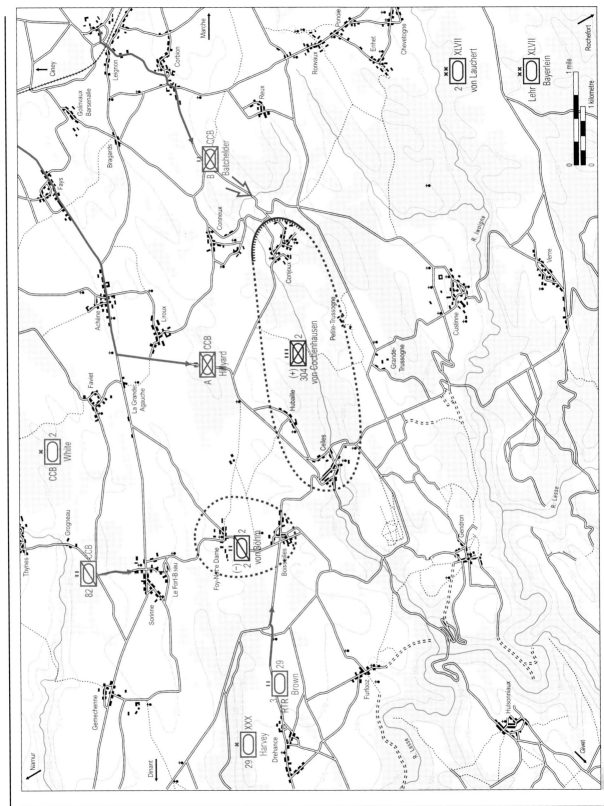

16/12/1944	17/12	18/12	19/12	20/12	21/12	22/12	23/12	24/12	25/12	26/12	27/12	28/12	29/12
pages 66-72	77-78	73-76	79-82,85-86	27-34,83-84	87-88,94-95	39-40		89-90					

For the counter-attack against the 2 Panzer Division pockets at Foy-Notre-Dame and Celles, Brigadier-General Isaac White's CCB/2nd Armored was split into two task forces which attacked from Achêne and Leignon, surrounding the Germans.

armour in the west which had forced British reconnaissance patrols to retire behind the Meuse at Dinant. The planned VII Corps attack was turning into a purely defensive battle, and the exact strength and location of the German battlegroups approaching the Meuse was speculative.

It is no wonder that Allied intelligence was confused at this point, because the analysts were actually trying to pinpoint the movements of four German Panzer divisions advancing almost parallel and sometimes overlapping: 2, 9, 116 and (130) Lehr. All had reconnaissance elements well out both to the front and the flanks, and were feeling their way around the American defences, probing for weak spots. This is why, for example, the leading Kampfgruppe of 2 Panzer Division, 'von Böhm', took a slightly different route towards Dinant to that of the following, much stronger, Kampfgruppe 'von Cochenhausen'. Marching by night, 2 Panzer's 'von Böhm' battlegroup

M4 Shermans of Major-General Ernest Harmon's 2nd Armored Division advance eastward from Celles after their Christmas victory. (Imperial War Museum)

had bumped into 2nd Armored Division patrols south of Ciney, forcing it to deviate.

The Panzer 'Lehr' Division, having come up behind and south of 2 Panzer Division, now overlapped its rear from the direction of Rochefort, while 116 was near Hotton and 9 still trying to get closer to the action but delayed through lack of fuel. The swarms of Allied fighters over the impending battlefields could not pass on any reliable information to the men on the ground because they had enough difficulty distinguishing friend from foe, let alone which German columns were exactly where. The pilot of a single-seater, flying low and at high speed, can't take down map references!

Harmon's decision to use CCB to attack what seemed to be the spearhead of the German forces, while CCA appeared to have things under control further east, was a calculated risk. However, he did not feel he could do so, having already risked CCA without permission, so in mid-afternoon he telephoned VII Corps' headquarters for an OK.

The following sequence of events is something of a comedy of errors. Lawton Collins was actually on his way to visit Harmon, and his deputy, Brigadier-General Williston Palmer, told Harmon to wait until he arrived. Moments after putting the phone down, Palmer received another call, this time from the First Army chief of staff, Major-General William Kean, who had been advised that Montgomery wanted to pull 2nd Armored back towards Andenne and Huy. Not

16/12/1944	17/12	18/12	19/12	20/12	21/12	22/12	23/12	24/12	25/12	26/12	27/12	28/12	29/12
pages 66-72	77-78	73-76	79-82,85-86	27-34,83-84	87-88,94-95	39-40		89-90					

Pockmarked, scarred and blistered, a PzKpfw IV and Panther from 2 Panzer Division's Kampfgruppe 'von Cochenhausen' destroyed in the battle around Celles.
(U.S. Signal Corps)

wanting to be too specific on an open line, Kean mentioned a 'pivoting move' towards towns 'A' and 'H' – which Palmer misinterpreted as Achêne and Houisse, just where Harmon wanted to send CCB. The phone line to Harmon had gone down, so Palmer sent a messenger telling Harmon to go ahead.

By this time, Lawton Collins had arrived at Harmon's command post and the two men began planning their attack for Christmas Day. Then Kean, perhaps sensing that Palmer may have misinterpreted him, phoned again to clarify his orders. Horrified, Palmer sent a second messenger chasing after the first. Collins nevertheless told Harmon to go ahead as planned. This was not the first time during the 'Battle of the Bulge' that a corps' commander had defied an order; Leonard Gerow had done the same to strengthen the defence of Elsenborn Ridge.

The attack began at 0800 hrs on 25 December. Harmon had split Brigadier-General Isaac White's CCB into two battlegroups. Task Force A, under Lieutenant-Colonel Harry Hillyard, was to attack from Achêne across the high ground northwest of Celles. Task Force B, under Major Clifton Batchelder, was to strike from Leignon and envelop the two 2 Panzer Division Kampfgruppen from the southeast. Simultan-eously, the 82nd Armored Reconnaissance Battalion was to attack towards Foy-Notre-Dame.

By mid-afternoon Task Force A had reached the high ground, losing three half-tracks but destroying three Panthers, while P-38s from the 370th Fighter Group accounted for four more. Task Force B brushed aside a small pocket of resistance in Conjoux and

reached the ridge southeast of Celles at about the same time. Meanwhile, the 82nd Reconnaissance Battalion had run into a fusilade of fire from Foy, but a combination of British artillery fire from the other side of the Meuse and another air attack took out Kampfgruppe 'von Böhm's four remaining Panthers, and the 82nd's light tanks and armoured cars made short work of the remaining defences. Some Germans managed to escape east to Celles, but the remaining 148, including the battlegroup commander, raised their hands in surrender.

Meanwhile, Hillyard's and Batchelder's two task forces had closed in on Celles, finding it virtually deserted apart from local villagers who had gathered in the illusory safety of the church. A couple of hundred dispirited Panzergrenadiers from Kampfgruppe 'von Cochenhausen' quickly gave up the unequal struggle, but CCB had completely missed the main force of the battlegroup, which was dispersed in the woods surrounding Celles. With darkness now falling, White told his two task force commanders to consolidate and finish mopping up in the morning.

The last act was soon over. American L-5 spotter aircraft drew down heavy and accurate artillery fire while P-38s attacked targets of opportunity. Then CCB's infantry and tanks advanced in a long sweep line, killing about 150 Germans and capturing another 200, alongside a mixed bag of vehicles and guns. About 800 got away, including von Cochenhausen, their commander, but the effective strength of 2 Panzer Division had been halved, for very few American casualties.

16/12/1944	17/12	18/12	19/12	20/12	21/12	22/12	23/12	24/12	25/12	26/12	27/12	28/12	29/12
pages 66-72	77-78	73-76	79-82,85-86	27-34,83-84	87-88,94-95	39-40		89-90					

U.S. VII CORPS' BATTLES

III/335th and 329th Infantry Regiments

Rochefort – December 22–29

On 29 December men of the 329th Regiment from Major-General Robert Macon's freshly arrived 83rd Infantry Division finally retook Rochefort. Newly transferred from XIX Corps of Ninth Army, with whom it had been battling around Winden only a couple of days earlier, the 83rd was the last major formation to join VII Corps in 1944, and only gets four mentions in all 720 pages of the U.S. official history of the battle! To set the record straight, therefore, it was the men of the 329th Infantry Regiment who forced the remnants of 2 Panzer Division to fall back during the night of 29/30 December, recaptured Malempré to the northeast of Hotton four days later and Langlir on 9 January, then kicked 9 SS-Panzer Division out of Courtil over the 17th-18th before being returned to XIX Corps.

Christmas Eve in Rochefort. After the battle, Fritz Bayerlein said that, 'owing to the exhaustion and heavy casualties of our attack forces, the pursuit had to be abandoned'. (U.S. Army)

Less than a week before its recapture by the 329th, the little town of Rochefort had suddenly assumed strategic importance because of its bridge over the river L'Homme which gives westward access north of the broader river Lesse towards Dinant. On 22 December the CO of the 84th Infantry Division, Brigadier-General Alexander Bolling, had put Company I of Major Gordon Bahe's 3rd Battalion, 335th Regiment, into Rochefort. Later, on corps orders, he sent the remainder of the battalion after them. This ran into a firefight with a German column at Marloie and had to detour, arriving in Rochefort early on the 23rd. But, apart from some shelling during the afternoon as Fritz Bayerlein deployed Panzer Lehr, the rest of the short daylight hours passed quietly.

In fact, Bayerlein was deceived into believing that the town was unoccupied, because there was no return artillery fire and a patrol he sent out reported it empty. One has to wonder how close the scouts really got, because from a single infantry company the morning before, the American garrison had swollen

16/12/1944	17/12	18/12	19/12	20/12	21/12	22/12	23/12	24/12	25/12	26/12	27/12	28/12	29/12
pages 66-72	77-78	73-76	79-82,85-86	27-34,83-84	87-88,94-95			35-38,89-90					

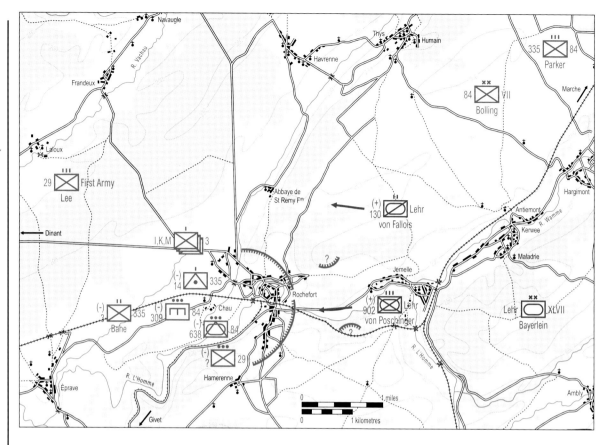

The capture of Rochefort, with its bridge over the river L'Homme giving access toward Givet and Dinant, was vital to Panzer Lehr, but their victory was shortlived.

considerably. Apart from Gordon Bahe's III/335th, plus two platoons from the regimental anti-tank company, it now also included a platoon of M18s from the division's attached 638th Tank Destroyer Battalion; a platoon of engineers from the 309th Battalion; and a solitary platoon from Major-General John Lee's 29th Separate Infantry Regiment, which had been tasked with guarding the radio repeater station at Jemelle, just to the east.

The defenders gave Panzer Lehr's leading battalion of 902 Panzergrenadier Regiment a hot time as it approached Rochefort down the defile of the St Hubert road. Expecting a walkover, the grenadiers were caught in crossfire and fell back in disorder. Now warned, Bayerlein planned his next attack more carefully, but again Gordon Bahe's men were waiting. The assault, by grenadiers supported by Panther tanks, began at 0200 hrs on Christmas Eve, and

Bayerlein later credited his opponents with courage as great as that shown at Bastogne.

The defence was concentrated around the Hôtel du Centre, where a pair of little 57mm anti-tank guns and half a dozen .50 machine-guns protected Bahe's command post. Elsewhere around the little town, GIs used every stone wall for shelter from the incessant machine-gun and mortar fire, and the fight became a close-quarters one from house to house. About 0900 hrs, Bahe's radio went on the blink, and the battle raged from street to street for another four hours before it was repaired and he received the welcome order from Bolling to withdraw.

Using the early nightfall as cover, Bahe's men 'made a concerted dash, firing wildly as they went and hurling smoke grenades'. The cost, for a 24-hour battle against far superior forces, was incredibly light: 25 dead and 15 wounded. No wonder a dispirited Panzergrenadier later chalked a message on an abandoned gun shield: 'Aus der Traum' – 'the dream is over'. It certainly was when the 329th Infantry Regiment retook Rochefort four days later.

16/12/1944	17/12	18/12	19/12	20/12	21/12	22/12	23/12	24/12	25/12	26/12	27/12	28/12	29/12
pages 66-72	77-78	73-76	79-82,85-86	27-34,83-84	87-88,94-95			35-38,89-90					

U.S. THIRD ARMY

P atton was probably better known to the American public during World War 2 than even Eisenhower or Marshall. His flamboyant showmanship and outspoken arrogance made him the darling of the media, to the frequent embarrassment of his superiors, and his rivalry with Montgomery became legendary. But it is not for these factors that soldiers remember him: it is for the unhesitant aggression and tireless drive which win battles. There are few better

Lieutenant-General George Patton was the American commander whose abilities were most respected by the Germans. He was not, however, always 'flavour of the month' with his peers. (U.S. Signal Corps)

U.S. THIRD ARMY
Lieutenant-General George Smith Patton, Jr.
Chief of Staff
Brigadier-General Hobart R. Gay

III Corps (Millikin)
VIII Corps (Middleton) (from First Army 20 December)
XII Corps (Eddy)
XX Corps (Walker) (to Seventh Army [Patch], 6th Army Group [Devers], 20 December)
109 Anti-Aircraft Gun Battalion (Mobile) (90mm)
115 Anti-Aircraft Gun Battalion (Mobile) (90mm)
217 Anti-Aircraft Gun Battalion (Mobile) (90mm)
456 Anti-Aircraft Artillery Auto-Weapons Battalion (40mm)
465 Anti-Aircraft Artillery Auto-Weapons Battalion (40mm)
550 Anti-Aircraft Artillery Auto-Weapons Battalion (40mm)
565 Anti-Aircraft Artillery Auto-Weapons Battalion (40mm)
777 Anti-Aircraft Artillery Auto-Weapons Battalion (M15/M16)
16 & 30 Bataillons Chasseurs (-), 2 Régiment Parachutistes (Puech-Samson) (French) (attached 21 December as liaison with British XXX Corps)

---

examples of this than the way in which he responded to the crisis in the Ardennes in December 1944.

Patton was one of the first men to see the ghastly risk (Bradley later called it 'calculated') of leaving the Ardennes so thinly manned. A diary entry from as early as 24 November reads: 'First Army is making a terrible mistake in leaving the VIII Corps static, as it is highly probable that the Germans are building up east of them'. Patton's G-2, Colonel Oscar Koch, shared his concern and by 9 December estimated that there were at least four infantry and two Panzer divisions facing Middleton's front, with three more close at hand.

Koch's warnings were listened to, then largely dismissed. The consensus was that the Germans, like the Americans, were using the sector to give depleted divisions a respite and new ones a limited taste of combat experience to acclimatise them. Even Patton,

with his sights firmly set on the Third Army's Saar offensive planned to begin on 19 December, began to think that those forces – if, indeed, they existed – east of the Ardennes would be used for spoiling attacks. From where they sat, they could either be launched north into the flank of First Army's offensive towards the Rur and Urft dams, scheduled to begin a few days before his own; or against Third Army's flank in the south. This would fit in with experiences in Normandy. SHAEF generally concurred that limited counter-attacks were likely, but that a major offensive was not, although Eisenhower confessed his worry about 'a nasty little Kasserine'.

George Smith Patton, Jr. was not, as he has sometimes been portrayed, like a bull in a china shop on the battlefield. His nickname, 'blood and guts' (for our blood, his guts) was not idle, and as many men

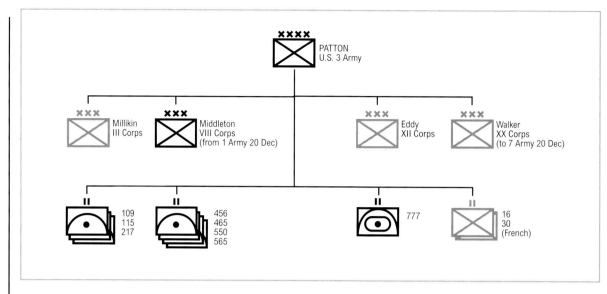

PATTON
U.S. 3 Army

Millikin
III Corps

Middleton
VIII Corps
(from 1 Army 20 Dec)

Eddy
XII Corps

Walker
XX Corps
(to 7 Army 20 Dec)

109
115
217

456
465
550
565

777

16
30
(French)

probably loathed him as loved him. But he did have the experience and the talent to win battles, and was the one Allied general whom the Germans feared most. It was partly for this reason that he had been given 'command' of the phantom army in East Anglia prior to D-Day, convincing Hitler that the assault would come in the Pas de Calais because Patton *had* to lead it.

In fact, of course, the invasion came in Normandy and the U.S. effort was spearheaded not by Patton's Third Army but by Bradley's First on 'Omaha' and 'Utah' beaches. Third Army did not get ashore until July and did not become operational until 1 August. At this point, Bradley moved up to become CO of 12th Army Group, his deputy, Courtney Hodges, taking over First Army. This gave Bradley parity with Montgomery, commander of 21st Army Group (Canadian First and British Second Armies) but

Montgomery would remain in overall command of all Allied ground forces for another month, until Eisenhower established SHAEF headquarters in France and assumed the responsibility himself – albeit 400 miles (640 km) behind the front line.

Originally Patton's Third Army was to have swept into Brittany to capture the major ports of St Malo, Brest and Lorient, but the German collapse after the 'Cobra' breakout through Avranches meant this was no longer necessary, and the task could be entrusted to VIII Corps from First Army instead. Patton's mission, exclusive of Brittany, was to drive to the river Mayenne and sweep the area south of First Army to the Loire. Major-General Wade Haislip's XV Corps headed through Avranches towards the Mayenne while Major-General Walton Walker's XX Corps reached Nantes and Angers on the Loire. By 8 August

A rather different Bastogne street scene to that shown earlier. Refugees straggle west out of the little town, already showing the scars of German shelling, before the siege which Patton's Third Army finally lifted.
(U.S. Signal Corps)

After the battle: refugees return to their town in January 1945 while jubilant American officers, including (centre) Major-General Maxwell Taylor, congratulate each other on survival and victory. (U.S. Signal Corps)

Haislip had reached Le Mans after a 75-mile (120-km) drive in just four days which had outflanked the German Seventh Armee.

The day before this, the Germans had launched a determined Panzer attack against the junction between First and Third Armies at Mortain. This penetrated VII Corps' lines but a massive air raid coupled with a counter-attack against the German flank by tanks from Lieutenant-General Henry Crerar's Canadian First Army sealed the Germans' fate and led to the encirclement at Falaise.

While part of Patton's XV Corps helped close the neck of the Falaise Pocket, other elements drove rapidly north through Dreux to secure crossings over the Seine at Mantes-Gassicourt on 19 August. Meanwhile, XX Corps had raced through Chartres on the 16th to capture Melun and Fontainbleau east of Paris on the 20th. Patton's third corps, XII, had since been brought into play and, after reaching Orléans on the 17th, was heading for Troyes. Originally commanded by Major-General Gilbert Cook, it was now led by the man who had commanded the 9th Infantry Division in Tunisia, Sicily and across 'Utah' beach, Major-General Manton Eddy.

Patton's Third Army rapidly outstripped the rest of 12th Army Group in the eastward drive across France after the various corps and divisions which had been intermingled around Falaise were sorted out. Soon, he was threatening Metz, but already a disconcerting gap was opening between First and Third Armies in September. In the middle lay the Ardennes. And Patton's tanks were running out of fuel, as the 'Mulberry' harbours in Normandy, almost demolished by a storm, could not cope with the load. The Channel ports that had been captured were also in a

severe state of disrepair, and could therefore only compensate partially.

Third Army got moving again on 5 September after replenishments finally reached them and, crossing the Meuse and advancing through Belgium and Luxembourg, finally reached the West Wall in October while First Army was fighting its own battle at Aachen and towards the river Rur. By this time Third Army had changed shape slightly because, after the battle of Falaise and the advance across the Seine, corps and divisions had become so mixed up that they had to be reorganised.

XV Corps had disappeared to become part of Patch's Seventh Army and in its place Patton now had Major-General John Millikin's III Corps. This included the 4th Armored Division, which would be rushed to Bastogne alongside the 26th Infantry Division plus the 80th, hastily transferred from Eddy's XII Corps because it was close. Millikin was a good choice for a variety of reasons to lead the Bastogne relief column, not least because – like Patton himself – he was a former cavalryman, and had commanded the 2nd (Horse) Cavalry Division at the time of Pearl Harbor before moving on.

After 20 December 1944 Patton also assumed control of Troy Middleton's VIII Corps from First Army. Third Army, thus reconstituted, remained part of Bradley's 12th Army Group, while First and Ninth became reluctant components in Montgomery's 21st Army Group. However, it was to prove a shortlived arrangement, because Eisenhower's agreement with 'Monty' was that it would cease as soon as Bastogne was safe and First and Third Armies joined hands. Here the story continues – Manton Eddy and John Millikin will have to wait their turn.

U.S. THIRD ARMY

U.S. VIII CORPS

When General der Panzertruppen Hasso von Manteuffel launched his Fifth Panzer Armee through the Schnee Eifel and across the river Our on 16 December 1944, he had three Korps, two of them Panzer, totalling nine divisions, four of them armoured. All that Major-General Troy Middleton had to oppose this might was three infantry divisions, one of them totally 'green' and the other two battle-weary and understrength, backed up by a single 'light' armoured division. The length of the line they held, some 85 miles (130 km), was far too

Mild-mannered and courteous to peers and subordinates alike, the bespectacled Troy Middleton was an experienced although unambitious commander who inspired loyalty from his men and fought hard on their behalf.
(U.S. Signal Corps)

long for them to defend adequately, and the Panzers and Volksgrenadiers had broken through quite decisively in several places within a couple of days.

The defence of St Vith, behind the line defended by the 106th Infantry Division on the north, or left flank, of Middleton's corps, was taken over by the newly arrived XVIII (Airborne) Corps' 7th Armored Division. The 4th Infantry Division in the south was absorbed by Patton's XII Corps. Only remnants of the 28th Infantry and 9th Armored Divisions remained to protect the centre – and the critical road junction at Bastogne – until the arrival of reinforcements. The most crucial of these in the first few days were the 101st Airborne Division from SHAEF reserve and Combat Command B from Patton's 10th Armored, which both converged

---

U.S VIII CORPS
Major-General Troy H. Middleton

4 Infantry Division (Barton)
　(to III Corps 20 December)
9 Armored Division (Leonard)
　(CCB attached to V Corps)
11 Armored Division (Kilburn)
　(from England 17-23 December)
17 Airborne Division (Miley)
　(from XVIII (Airborne) Corps 1 January 1945)
28 Infantry Division (Cota)
　(112 Infantry Regiment to V Corps 20 December)
87 Infantry Division (Culin)
　(from XV Corps 28-29 December)
101 Airborne Division (McAuliffe pp Taylor)
　(from SHAEF Reserve 17 December)
106 Infantry Division (Jones/Perrin)
　(survivors to V Corps 20 December)
CCB, 10 Armored Division (Roberts)
14 Cavalry Group1 Mechanized (Devine/Duggan):
　18 & 32 Cavalry Reconnaissance Squadrons
70 Tank Battalion (Davidson)
707 Tank Battalion
630 Tank Destroyer Battalion (A Company towed; B & C M36)
802 Tank Destroyer Battalion (towed)
803 Tank Destroyer Battalion (M10/M36)
811 Tank Destroyer Battalion (-) (M18)
820 Tank Destroyer Battalion (M18)
174 Field Artillery Group: 965, 969 & 770
　Field Artillery Battalions
333 Field Artillery Group: 333 & 771
　Field Artillery Battalions
402 Field Artillery Group: 559, 561 & 740
　Field Artillery Battalions
422 Field Artillery Group: 81 & 174 Field Artillery Battalions
687 Field Artillery Battalion

---

on Bastogne to deny it to the enemy in the face of overwhelming odds.

VIII Corps' commander, Troy Middleton, mild and bespectacled, was regarded by some of his peers as a 'plodder', but was tireless, resourceful and not given to panic. In November 1943 he had commanded the

U.S VIII CORPS – continued

447 Anti-Aircraft Artillery Auto-Weapons Battalion (M15/M16)
635 Anti-Aircraft Artillery Auto-Weapons Battalion (40mm)
778 Anti-Aircraft Artillery Auto-Weapons Battalion (40mm)
1102 Engineer Group: 341 Engineer General Service Battalion
1107 Engineer Combat Group: 159, 168 (Nungesser)
1128 Engineer Combat Group: 35, 44 & 158 Engineer
  Combat Battalions
178 Engineer Combat Battalion
249 Engineer Combat Battalion

U.S. VIII CORPS TROOPS

174 Field Artillery Group
770 Field Artillery Battalion (12 x 4.5" M1 gun, tractor-drawn)
965 Field Artillery Battalion (12 x 155mm M1A1 howitzer,
  tractor-drawn)
969 Field Artillery Battalion (Colored) (12 x 155mm M1A1
  howitzer, tractor-drawn)

333 Field Artillery Group
333 Field Artillery Battalion (Colored) (12 x 155mm M1A1
  howitzer, tractor-drawn)
771 Field Artillery Battalion (12 x 4.5" M1 gun, tractor-drawn)

402 Field Artillery Group
559 Field Artillery Battalion (12 x 155mm M1 gun,
  truck-drawn)
561 Field Artillery Battalion (12 x 155mm M1 gun,
  truck-drawn)
740 Field Artillery Battalion (12 x 8" M1 howitzer, tractor-
drawn)

422 Field Artillery Group
81 Field Artillery Battalion (12 x 155mm M1A1 howitzer,
  tractor-drawn)
174 Field Artillery Battalion (12 x 155mm M12 GMC)

Field Artillery Battalions
687 (12 x 105mm M2A1 howitzer, truck-drawn)

45th Infantry Division during its crossing of the river Volturno in Italy, a 10-day battle under atrocious conditions which proved he was no 'slouch'. He was rewarded with command of VIII Corps which came ashore across 'Utah' beach in the second wave of the Normandy landings. It spearheaded the breakout from the base of the Cotentin peninsula across the Carentan Plain in July 1944, reaching Avranches on the 30th before swinging right into Britanny, with its major ports of St Malo, Brest and Lorient.

Middleton drove his corps on through France and Belgium until his divisions reached the proximity of the West Wall in October/November. At this time the corps found itself in the centre of First Army's eastward march with, in effect, little to do. The Ardennes had been cleared of opposition and salients – albeit shallow ones – established through the West Wall in front of the Schnee Eifel and at Sevenig a little further south. The main effort was being put in north and south, with drives towards the Rur and Urft dams, and the Saar, respectively. The VIII Corps' sector was thus regarded as a quiet region where battle-weary troops could recuperate and those new to the European theatre of operations could acclimatise. In fact, the corps mission was, in the words of the U.S. official history, to 'train, rest, re-equip and observe the enemy'.

Allied planners totally misread German intentions, although both Eisenhower and his chief of intelligence,

Typifying the weakness of VIII Corps' sector, an M5 Stuart light tank escorts a convoy of 'soft-skin' vehicles westward while a trio of GIs wait, apparently impassively, for the Germans who will soon follow. (U.S. Signal Corps)

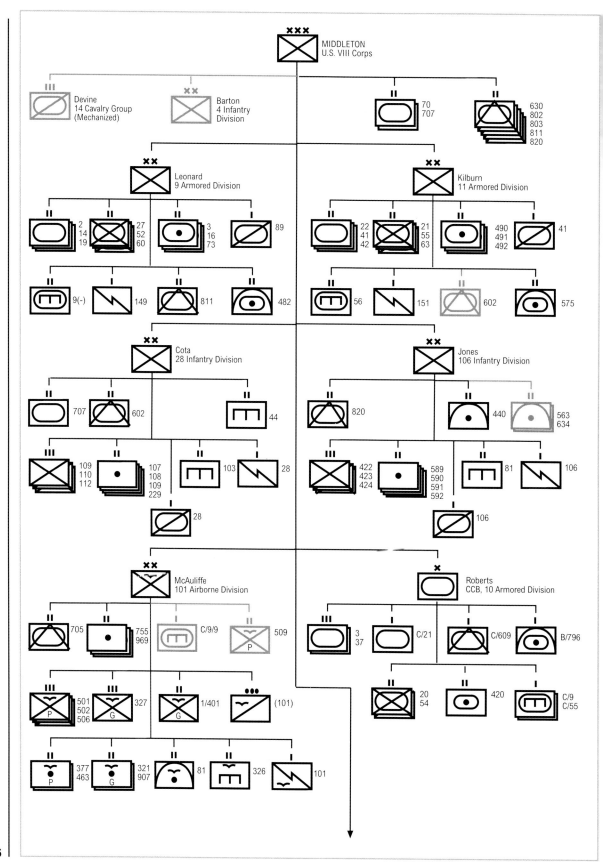

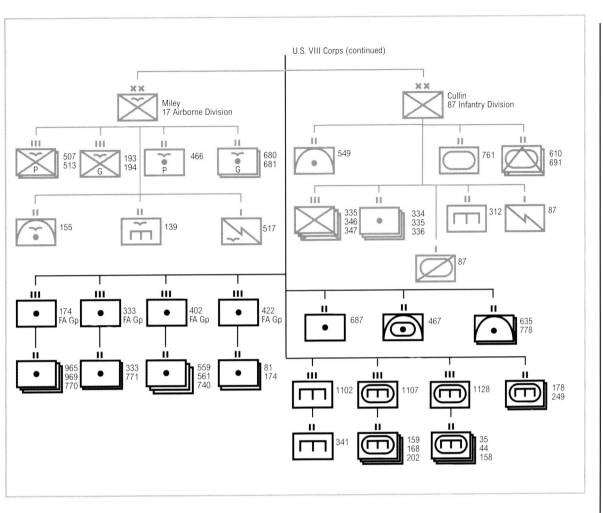

Major-General Kenneth Strong, were worried about the possibility of a spoiling attack to disrupt the Rur/Urft offensive. They did not expect at all the major onslaught which reduced VIII Corps to tatters.

In the north, Volksgrenadiers exploited the gap caused by the premature withdrawal of the 14th Cavalry Group to outflank and envelop two of the 106th Infantry Division's regiments and go on, helped by the arrival of the élite Führer Begleit Brigade, to capture St Vith. In the centre, the 110th Regiment of the 28th Infantry Division was overwhelmed – although not without a determined and effective struggle – while its two flanking regiments had to give ground steadily, retiring northwest and southwest respectively. In the south, only one regiment of the 4th Infantry Division was affected at first, around Echternach, and fought a series of company-sized actions which bought time for swift retaliation.

Seeing what was happening within hours of the German attack, Troy Middleton quite sensibly and honourably appealed to his army commander, Courtney Hodges, for help. In particular, he asked for

tanks, and the 7th Armored Division was ordered to St Vith. Patton similarly detached a combat command from 10th Armored Division towards Bastogne, and more would follow as rapidly as the road and weather conditions permitted over the next few days. But Middleton's corps was only saved by a hair's breadth and the sheer guts and determination of small groups of GIs shivering in frozen foxholes or sheltering behind snow-laden trees which turned the whole landscape into a Teutonic mythological nightmare.

Troy Middleton played little part in directing the course of the battle, other than by informing others of what appeared to be happening. This is no reflection on his abilities. Few could have done so much to keep tabs on such a confused and constantly shifting battlefield. But there are limits and, in fact, when Patton visited Middleton on 20 December, he reported that the corps was 'in such shape that it could not be used offensively'. What Middleton and the men under his command did achieve was to cause the Germans sufficient delay, particularly east of Bastogne, that all their subsequent efforts proved ultimately futile.

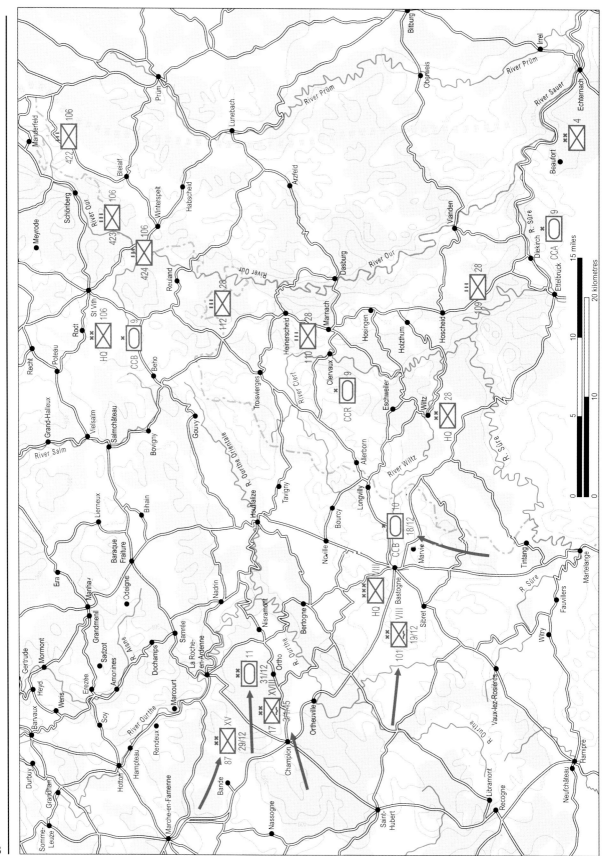

9th Armored Division

The unfortunate 9th Armored Division found its three combat commands widely dispersed down almost the whole of VIII Corps' front when the German offensive opened on 16 December. Furthest north, Brigadier-General William Hoge's CCB was rushed to St Vith, where to all intents and purposes it became part of V and then XVIII (Airborne) Corps. In the centre, Colonel Joseph Gilbreth's CCR became involved in the defence of Bastogne. Furthest south and east, Colonel Thomas Harrold's CCA around Savelborn virtually became part of Patton's XII Corps.

The 'bulge' was, in fact, 9th Armored's first battle and, under the circumstances, Major-General John Leonard's men acquitted themselves well – as did

Major-General John Leonard (profile, left) confers with his corps commander, Troy Middleton, before the battle, some time in November. Also present at this meeting were Eisenhower and Bradley. (U.S. Army)

9th ARMORED DIVISION
Major-General John W. Leonard
HQ Company and HQ Companies,
Combat Commands
A *(Harrold)*, B *(Hoge* – attached to V Corps)
& R *(Gilbreth)*

---

2 Tank Battalion (Harper)
14 Tank Battalion (Engemann)
19 Tank Battalion (Harrold)
27 Armored Infantry Battalion (Seeley)
52 Armored Infantry Battalion (Booth)
60 Armored Infantry Battalion (Collins)
3 Armored Field Artillery Battalion (M7)
16 Armored Field Artillery Battalion (M7)
73 Armored Field Artillery Battalion (M7)
89 Cavalry Reconnaissance Squadron, Mechanized
9 Armored Engineer Battalion
  (- C Company attached to CCB, 10 Armored Division)
2 Medical Battalion, Armored
149 Armored Signal Company
131 Armored Ordnance Maintenance Battalion
Military Police Platoon
482 Anti-Aircraft Artillery Auto-Weapons Battalion (M15/M16)
  (attached)
811 Tank Destroyer Battalion (M18) (attached)

---

many other newcomers to the European battlefield during this last desperate gamble of Hitler to regain the initiative in the west. (Three months later, the men of 9th Armored would win undying fame and even have a Hollywood film made about their exploits, but for the moment their thoughts were far from California!)

The division had been activated at Fort Riley, Kansas, on 15 July 1942 under Major-General Geoffrey Keyes. John Leonard took over in October the same year and remained in command until the end

The thin line held loosely by Middleton's 106th and, in particular, 28th Infantry Divisions on 16 December is clearly apparent from the scale of the map. The arrival of CCB from Patton's 10th Armored Division and that of the 101st Airborne from SHAEF reserve came just in time to retrieve victory from disaster.

of the war in Europe. The division was originally earmarked for III Corps of Ninth Army, but after it arrived in France on 3 October 1944 it was reassigned to VIII Corps and its components given a roughly 40-mile (60-km) stretch of front to patrol.

When the German offensive broke on 16 December, Hoge's CCB was on loan to V Corps, deployed around Faymonville in readiness to support the 2nd Infantry Division's attack through the West Wall at Wahlerscheid towards the Rur and Urft dams. When this operation was called off in response to the emergency and 2nd Infantry redeployed on Elsenborn Ridge, First Army commander Courtney Hodges placed CCB under the command of the 106th Infantry Division, which occupied positions in the Schnee Eifel recently vacated by the 2nd Infantry Division.

The CO of the 106th, Major-General Alan Jones,

initially wanted to use Hoge's tanks to counter-attack towards Schönberg, but when he heard that the whole of 7th Armored Division was also on its way to his aid, he postponed the plan. In fact, it never happened because, when 7th Armored's CCB commander, Brigadier-General Bruce Clarke, took over the defence of St Vith, the situation had deteriorated to such a point that it would have been futile. Instead, he deployed Hoge's tanks to the southeast of St Vith with his own completing a 'horseshoe' defence into which the survivors of the 106th could retire.

Meanwhile, Gilbreth's CCR had been deployed as a backstop for the 28th Infantry Division on 'Skyline Drive' but, split into 'penny packet' task forces, was unable to do more than help to hinder Fifth Panzer Armee's advance, and the survivors filtered back towards Bastogne, where they joined CCB of 10th Armored Division as CCX under command of the 101st Airborne Division. Harrold's CCA, down south in the Ermsdorf–Savelborn area on the left flank of 4th Infantry Division, facing only a single poorly equipped Volksgrenadier Division, had a much easier time of it.

On 30 December, after the evacuation of St Vith and the relief of Bastogne by Patton's forces, the component commands of 9th Armored were pulled back into reserve at Sedan and took no part in the Allied counter-offensive in January 1945. Instead, the division received replacements for its casualties and spent February retraining before attacking across the river Rur through Wollersheim and Langendorf on 2 March. Two days later the division was on the west bank of the river Erft around Euskirchen and on the 5th launched an offensive towards the confluence of the rivers Ahr and Rhein.

On 7 March an astonished platoon of CCR commanded by Lieutenant Emmet Burrows reached the heights overlooking the Rhein at Remagen, to see a rail bridge miraculously still intact. As soon as he heard the news, CCB commander William Hoge reacted promptly and sent tanks plunging down the slope to capture the bridge before the astonished Germans could destroy it. Their demolition charges were set off belatedly, but the bridge still stood and the delighted Americans charged across. Even though Remagen was far from where the main Rhein crossings were to take place later in the month, Eisenhower told Bradley to put at least five divisions across and hold a bridgehead. (The Ludendorff bridge actually collapsed on 17 March but by this time pontoons had taken over most of the load.)

After consolidating the bridgehead, 9th Armored renewed its eastward drive on the 26th, reached the river Lahn, established contact with Third Army on the Frankfurt–Köln autobahn and, by the end of the month, had established another bridgehead across the river Diemel near Warburg. Moving up to a new assembly area east of the river Weser on 8 April, the division spearheaded the drive towards the river Saale, consolidating near Pegau on the 13th. German resistance was intensifying all the time as the desperate troops found themselves in between the closing jaws of the Red Army and the western Allies, and 9th Armored struggled through factory districts at

Tiny specks in a desolate landscape, a troop of Shermans from 9th Armored Division's CCR deployed on a ridge to help cover the retreat of survivors from the 28th Infantry Division. (U.S. Signal Corps)

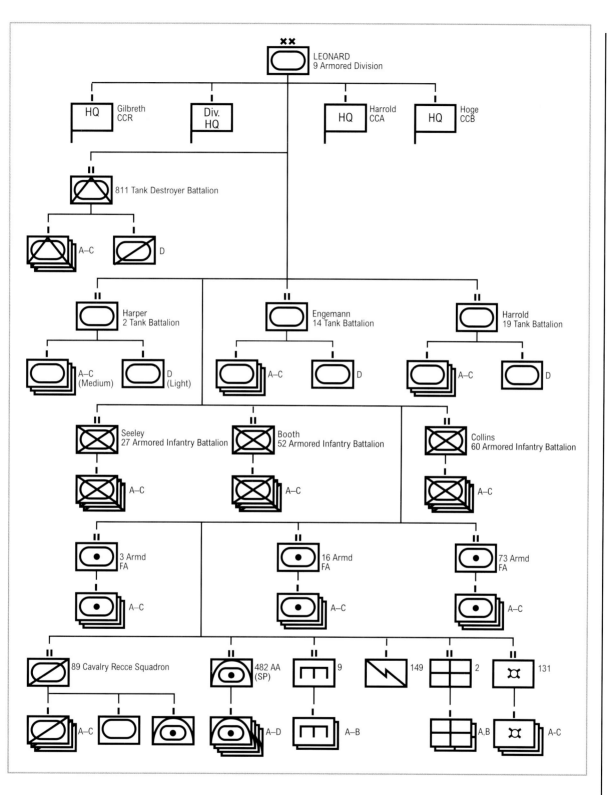

Deutzen before CCR reached the river Mulde and seized bridges in the Lastau region on the 15th. Next day it crossed the river and captured Colditz with its mountain-top PoW fortress.

After mopping up along the Mulde, the division was taken into reserve on 21 April and moved to Jena. It did not fight as a whole again, but CCA was attached to the 1st Infantry Division on 3 May for the drive towards Karlsbad and its famous caverns, and had reached Rudolec when hostilities ended on the 7th.

11th Armored Division
'Thunderbolt'

The 11th Armored Division had a very short war as it did not land in France until 17 December 1944, and lost 'only' 522 men in five months of combat. Immediately thrown into the 'Battle of the Bulge' as a mobile reserve for VIII Corps, it was moved up to the Neufchâteau region between 23-29 December and found the going difficult as it battled alongside the almost equally inexperienced 87th Infantry Division towards Houffalize over the next few days.

The division had not been activated until 15 August 1942, at Camp Polk, Louisiana. Its first commander was Major-General Edward Brooks, who later led 2nd Armored Division ashore in Normandy in June 1944. Brooks had been succeeded as CO of the 11th earlier in the year by Charles Kilburn, who led it until March 1945 before himself bring succeeded by Major-General Holmes Dager.

During the Ardennes offensive, CCB attacked Chenogne on 31 December and captured Senochamps on 2 January, while CCR assaulted Acul and CCA drove east of Rechrival. Thrown into the defence of the Bastogne corridor over the next 10 days, the division surrounded the German garrison in Bertogne on the 13th, but CCA was forced back from Velleroux by a determined counter-attack on the 15th. Next day, Brigadier-General Willard Holbrook's command stormed the village and retook it. Taking up positions on the line Bourcy–Hardigny, the division pursued the retreating Germans from 20 January, crossed into Luxembourg on the 22nd and relieved the 90th Infantry Division on the river Our over 4-5 February.

A patrol from the 11th Armored Division gingerly paddles across the icy river Ourthe. (U.S. Army)

11th ARMORED DIVISION
Major-General Charles S. Kilburn
HQ Company and HQ Companies,
Combat Commands A *(Holbrook)*, B *(Yale)* & R *(Bell)*

22 Tank Battalion
41 Tank Battalion (Sagaser)
42 Tank Battalion
21 Armored Infantry Battalion
55 Armored Infantry Battalion
63 Armored Infantry Battalion
490 Armored Field Artillery Battalion (M7)
491 Armored Field Artillery Battalion (M7)
492 Armored Field Artillery Battalion (M7)
41 Cavalry Reconnaissance Squadron, Mechanized
56 Armored Engineer Battalion
81 Medical Battalion, Armored
151 Armored Signal Company
133 Armored Ordnance Maintenance Battalion
Military Police Platoon
575 Anti-Aircraft Artillery Auto-Weapons Battalion (M15/M16)
  (attached 23 December)
602 Tank Destroyer Battalion (M18)
  (from 28 Infantry Division 29 December)

An attack against the West Wall on the 6th was only a partial success, but on the 18th a surprise assault won through and CCR captured Herzfeld. Sengerich, Roscheid, Eschfeld and Reiff fell in quick succession, then CCA assisted the 87th Infantry Division in its assault through the heavily defended West Wall pillboxes and other obstacles around Ormont at the end of the month. CCB next crossed the river Pruem and attacked through light resistance towards the river Kyll, which it reached on 4 March near Lissingen. Five days later the division had reached the Rhein and on the 21st completed the capture of the city of Worms.

Now commanded by Holmes Dager and reassigned to XII Corps, the 11th Armored moved to Hanau on the river Main at the end of the month and attacked through the lines of the 26th Infantry Division towards the Fulda Gap, battling through the Thuringer Wald at the beginning of April. On the 10th the division attacked the city of Coburg, which fell next day, before establishing bridgeheads over the river Hasslach at

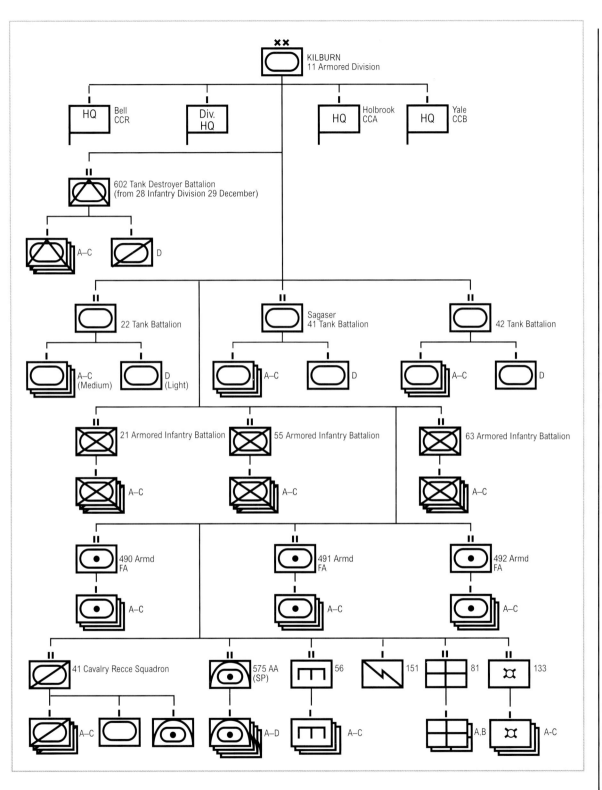

Kronach and Marktzeuln. Bayreuth surrendered on 14 April, then 11th Armored relieved the 71st Infantry Division and attacked to capture Grafenwohr on the 19th. Kreuzberg fell on the 25th and the division advanced rapidly towards the Austrian border, capturing Wegscheiden on the 30th after a major battle. On 5 May the 11th Armored Division captured Linz and established contact with Red Army troops at Amstetten the day after hostilities ended, 8 May.

28th Infantry Division
'Keystone'

The 28th well and truly lived up to its nickname in December 1944 because it really was the 'keystone' of the defence in the centre of VIII Corps' front, and its defence of the Our and Clerf crossings on 'Skyline Drive' bought the vital time needed to reinforce Bastogne and deny this pivotal town to the Germans. The 25-mile (40-km) front held by Major-General Norman Cota's three infantry regiments, battered and understrength after their long ordeal in the Hürtgen Forest, was too long to defend in any depth. As a result, Cota used individual villages as strongpoints, establishing a form of 'hedgehog' defence. He also had CCR of 9th Armored Division as a backstop. That this was inadequate to stop a determined assault was known to everyone from Bradley down – but this was the 'quiet' front...

Omar Bradley had, in fact, a soft spot for the 28th, because he had commanded it during 1942-43. Originally a Pennsylvania National Guard formation, the division was inducted into Federal service on 17 February 1941 at Philadelphia, but did not see action until, as part of XIX Corps, Third Army, it landed in France on 22 July 1944. Its commander, Major-General Lloyd Brown, was killed during the

28th INFANTRY DIVISION
Major-General Norman D. Cota
HQ Company

109 Infantry Regiment (Rudder)
110 Infantry Regiment (Fuller)
112 Infantry Regiment (Nelson) (to V Corps 20 December)
107 Field Artillery Battalion (105mm)
108 Field Artillery Battalion (155mm)
109 Field Artillery Battalion (105mm)
229 Field Artillery Battalion (105mm)
28 Reconnaissance Troop, Mechanized
103 Engineer Combat Battalion
103 Medical Battalion
28 Signal Company
28 Quartermaster Company
728 Ordnance Light Maintenance Company
Military Police Platoon
707 Tank Battalion (attached)
602 Tank Destroyer Battalion (M18)
  (attached 24-29 December)
44 Engineer Combat Battalion (Kjeldsetb)
  (attached from corps reserve 18 December)

Major-General Norman Cota enjoys a rare moment of relaxation before he and his men were thrown into the battles of the Hürtgen Forest and 'Skyline Drive'. (U.S. Army)

bocage fighting north and west of St Lô on 12 August. Norman Cota succeeded him for the rest of the war.

Now reassigned to V Corps, the division paraded through Paris on 29 August before crossing the river Oise northeast of the capital two days later. Continuing across France, Belgium and Luxembourg, it entered Germany near Binfeld on 11 September and attacked the West Wall at Grosskampenberg. After a two-day

battle the 28th broke through and captured Roscheid, but then German resistance caused the offensive to grind to a halt.

After containing counter attacks, the division was moved north to Elsenborn on 1 October. At the end of the month the 28th relieved the 9th Infantry Division and on 2 November launched an attack towards Schmidt through the Hürtgen Forest. The official U.S. history describes the following fighting as 'one of the most costly division actions in the whole of World War II', with the small villages of Vossenack and Schmidt changing hands several times.

Reassigned to VIII Corps and given a 'quiet' sector of front in which to recuperate, the division suffered further heavy losses during the 'battle of the bulge' and the survivors were pulled back behind the Meuse. The reconstituted division was reassigned to XXI Corps and helped in the capture of Colmar at the beginning of February 1945. Advancing alongside French armour, the division reached the river Ahr in early March and saw no further action.

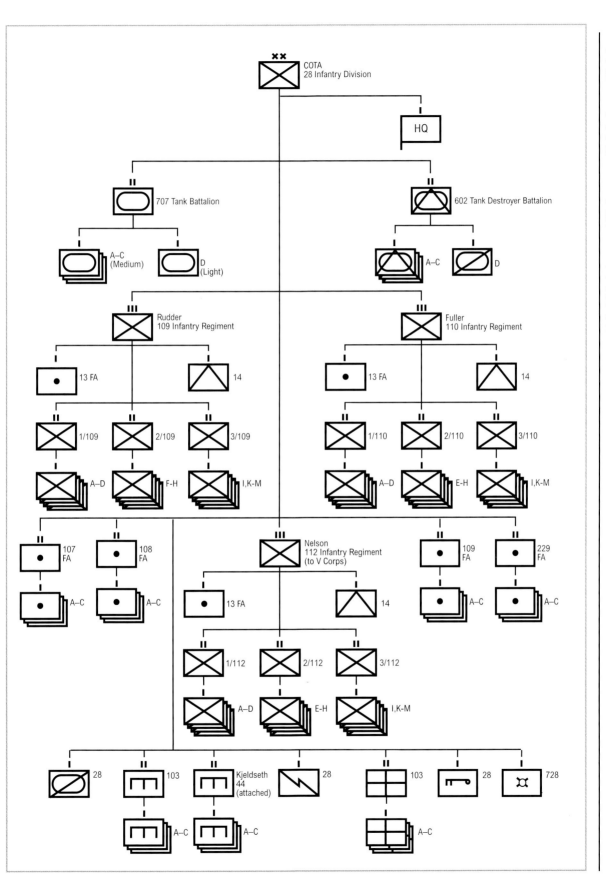

COTA
28 Infantry Division

HQ

707 Tank Battalion

602 Tank Destroyer Battalion

A–C
(Medium)

D
(Light)

A–C

D

Rudder
109 Infantry Regiment

13 FA

14

Fuller
110 Infantry Regiment

13 FA

14

1/109

2/109

3/109

1/110

2/110

3/110

A–D

F-H

I,K-M

A–D

E-H

I,K-M

107
FA

108
FA

Nelson
112 Infantry Regiment
(to V Corps)

109
FA

229
FA

A–C

A–C

13 FA

14

A–C

A–C

1/112

2/112

3/112

A–D

E-H

I,K-M

28

103

Kjeldseth
44
(attached)

28

103

28

728

A–C

A–C

A–C

87th Infantry Division

'Golden Acorn'

Major-General Frank Culin's 87th had landed in France only at the beginning of December 1944 and, assigned to Manton Eddy's XII Corps, moved up to the Saar-German border for Third Army's planned offensive. The division had begun its attack through the West Wall on 14 December and captured Rimling and Oberailbrach after a fierce fight before operations were halted on the 18th in response to the German Ardennes offensive. The division was taken into SHAEF reserve on the 24th and five days later, reassigned to VIII Corps, it re-assembled between Bertrix and Libramont, entrusted, alongside the 11th Armored Division, with the southern hook to rejoin First and Third Armies.

The division had been activated at Camp McCain, Missouri, on 15 December 1942 under Major-General Percy Clarkson. Commanded since April 1944 by Frank Culin, it shipped to England in November and arrived on the Continent on 5 December. Now, nearly four weeks later, it had an important role to play in re-establishing the front and driving the Germans back behind their start lines for Operation 'Herbstnebel'.

On the morning of 30 December the 345th and 346th Infantry Regiments trucked north to their start line near Bras, their first objective to sever the German supply route between St Hubert and Bastogne. They took Moircy later in the day, then lost it to a counter-attack on New Year's Eve, but recaptured it on 1 January. Further seesaw battles east of St Hubert at Bonnerue and Tillet over the next 10 days took the

Triumphant GIs of Culin's 87th Infantry Division meet up with a British patrol in a village on the banks of the river Ourthe. (Imperial War Museum)

87th INFANTRY DIVISION
Major-General Frank L. Culin
HQ Company

---

345 Infantry Regiment (Sugg)
346 Infantry Regiment (Wheeler)
347 Infantry Regiment (Tupper)
334 Field Artillery Battalion (105mm)
335 Field Artillery Battalion (155mm)
336 Field Artillery Battalion (105mm)
912 Field Artillery Battalion (105mm)
87 Reconnaissance Troop, Mechanized
312 Enginer Combat Battalion
312 Medical Battalion
87 Signal Company
87 Quartermaster Company
787 Ordnance Light Maintenance Company
Military Police Platoon
549 Anti-Aircraft Artillery Auto-Weapons Battalion (40mm)
   (attached 24 December)
761 Tank Battalion (Colored) (George)
   (attached 20-23 December)
610 Tank Destroyer Battalion (M36) (detached 22 December)
691 Tank Destroyer Battalion (M36) (attached 22 December)

---

division across the river Ronce and up to the Ourthe, where it made contact with British forces.

Transferred back to XII Corps next day, the division relieved the 4th Infantry on the Sauer south of Echternach and captured Wasserbilling on the 23rd. The transfer was shortlived because, on the 25th, the division reverted to VIII Corps. The 87th relieved the 17th Airborne on the 26th and took over the St Vith sector. Attacking across the river Our through the West Wall at the end of the month, the division took Manderfeld and Auw, fought the battle for the 'Schnee Eifel Crossroads' east of Kobscheid over 6–7 February, and then went over to the defensive.

The division returned to the attack at the end of the month, helping capture Ormont and seizing a bridge over the river Ahr on 8 March. In the middle of the month it reached the Mosel and, after fierce hand-to-hand fighting, captured Koblenz and the imposing Fort Constantine. The division crossed the Rhein on the 25th, helped clear the Thuringer Wald during April and ended the war on the Czech border at Falkenstein.

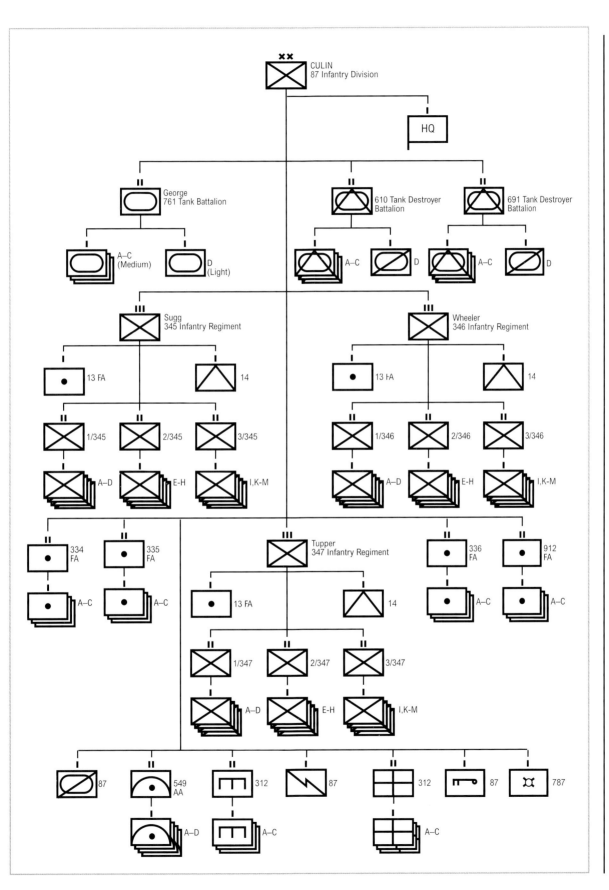

CULIN
87 Infantry Division

HQ

George
761 Tank Battalion

610 Tank Destroyer
Battalion

691 Tank Destroyer
Battalion

A–C
(Medium)

D
(Light)

A–C

D

A–C

D

Sugg
345 Infantry Regiment

Wheeler
346 Infantry Regiment

13 FA

14

13 FA

14

1/345

2/345

3/345

1/346

2/346

3/346

A–D

E–H

I,K-M

A–D

E–H

I,K-M

334
FA

335
FA

Tupper
347 Infantry Regiment

336
FA

912
FA

A–C

A–C

13 FA

14

A–C

A–C

1/347

2/347

3/347

A–D

E–H

I,K-M

87

549
AA

312

87

312

87

787

A–D

A–C

A–C

106th Infantry Division
'Golden Lions'

The 106th had only newly arrived in Europe on 6 December and its commander, Alan Jones, was not at all happy about the position it was placed in when he relieved Major-General Walter Robertson's 2nd Infantry Division in the Schnee Eifel. This broad but shallow salient east of the West Wall, with its wooded valleys and hillsides, was a tempting target for a German counter-attack, and Jones' fears were to be realised all too soon.

The 106th was the last of the 66 U.S. infantry divisions to be activated during World War 2. Formed on 15 March 1943 at Fort Jackson, South Carolina, under Alan Jones, it was one of those unfortunate higher-numbered divisions whose ranks had been repeatedly stripped to provide replacements ('reinforcements') for

Major-General Alan Jones was one of the victims of the 'Battle of the Bulge'. Unable to cope with the situation, he sought reassurance rather than responsibility and had to be relieved of command.
(U.S. Signal Corps)

106th INFANTRY DIVISION
Major-General Alan W.Jones/
Brigadier-General Herbert T. Perrin
HQ Company

---

422 Infantry Regiment (Deschenaux)
423 Infantry Regiment (Cavender)
424 Infantry Regiment (Reid)
589 Field Artillery Battalion (-) (105mm)
590 Field Artillery Battalion (105mm)
591 Field Artillery Battalion 105mm)
592 Field Artillery Battalion (155mm)
106 Reconnaissance Troop, Mechanized
81 Engineer Combat Battalion (Riggs, see OOB 5)
331 Medical Battalion
106 Signal Company
106 Quartermaster Company
806 Ordnance Light Maintenance Company
Military Police Platoon
440 Anti-Aircraft Artillery Auto-Weapons Battalion (40mm)
  (attached 17 December)
563 Anti-Aircraft Artillery Auto-Weapons Battalion (40mm)
  (detached 18 December)
634 Anti-Aircraft Artillery Auto-Weapons Battalion (40mm)
  (detached 18 December)
820 Tank Destroyer Battalion (M18) (attached)

---

other divisions. When it departed from Boston on 10 November 1944, most of its men were only partially trained, but, unlike the equally raw 99th Infantry Division on Elsenborn Ridge, they were unable to withstand the German onslaught. The result was the worst American defeat in the whole of the European campaign, with 6,697 men entering German captivity (of whom 6,500 survived).

To add insult to injury, the attack on the Schnee Eifel and the subsequent assault on St Vith were almost afterthoughts in German planning, designed just to close the gap between Fifth and Sixth Panzer Armees. But, due to bad luck for the 106th, the Volksgrenadiers were able to exploit the breach created by the withdrawal of the 14th Cavalry Group in the Losheim Gap and surround the unfortunate 422nd and 423rd Infantry Regiments before there were sufficient reserves for a counter-attack to rescue them.

Only the 424th Regiment, furthest south at Winterspelt, and elements of the 820th Tank Destroyer Battalion, escaped westward to friendly lines.

After the evacuation of St Vith the 424th, attached to 7th Armored Division, fought at Manhay before being withdrawn to Belgium. As an interim measure, the unattached 517th Parachute Infantry Regiment was added to the 424th to constitute a 'new' 106th under Alan Jones' deputy, Brigadier-General Herbert Perrin. This arrangement was shortlived and the 424th was re-attached to 7th Armored during the recapture of St Vith in January 1945, fighting at Meyrode. Briefly attached to the 99th Infantry Division in February, the 424th was withdrawn to St Quentin in March, where the 3rd and 159th Infantry Regiments replaced the captured units. However, the 106th saw no further action and was, with black humour, relegated to processing German prisoners for the rest of the war.

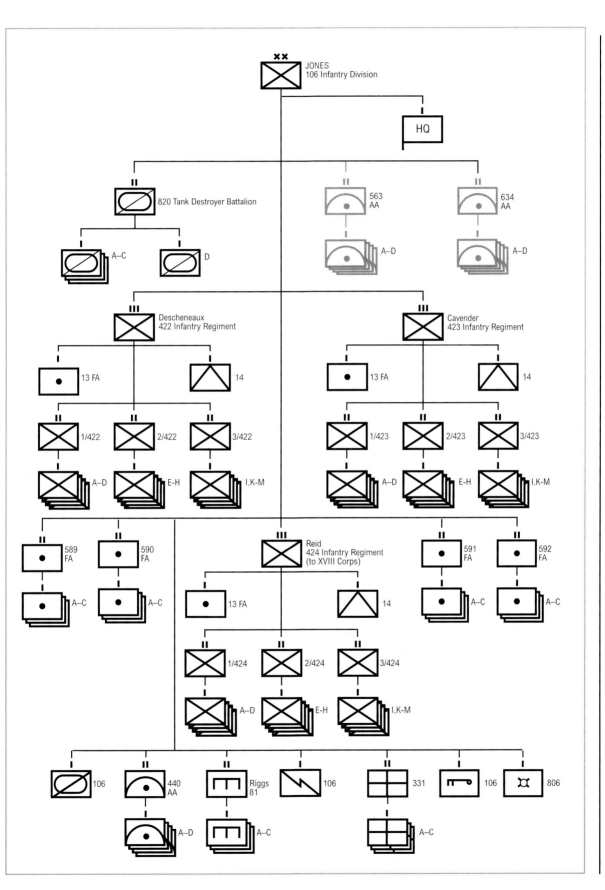

XX
JONES
106 Infantry Division

HQ

820 Tank Destroyer Battalion

A–C

D

563
AA

A–D

634
AA

A–D

Descheneaux
422 Infantry Regiment

13 FA

14

1/422

2/422

3/422

A–D

E-H

I,K-M

Cavender
423 Infantry Regiment

13 FA

14

1/423

2/423

3/423

A–D

E-H

I,K-M

589
FA

A–C

590
FA

A–C

Reid
424 Infantry Regiment
(to XVIII Corps)

13 FA

14

1/424

2/424

3/424

A–D

E-H

I,K-M

591
FA

A–C

592
FA

A–C

106

440
AA

A–D

Riggs
81

A–C

106

331

A–C

106

806

17th Airborne Division

'Golden Talon'

On 16 December 1944 Major-General William Miley's untried division was still in England, being inspected by the CO of XVIII (Airborne) Corps, Matthew Ridgway, to ensure its readiness for battle. Two days after the beginning of the German offensive, Eisenhower ordered both it and the 11th Armored Division, which had just arrived in France, to proceed to the Meuse without delay. (Ridgway himself had already flown post-haste to join his deputy, James Gavin, in the 82nd Airborne headquarters at Werbomont.)

The division had been activated under Miley's command on 15 April 1943 at Camp Mackall, North Carolina (named after one of the U.S. airborne corps' first fatal battle casualties during Operation 'Torch'). The 17th arrived in England in August 1944 and was flown by emergency night flights to Reims over 23–25 December, bad weather having grounded its C-47s earlier than this. It immediately moved by road to Charleville, but the threat of the Germans actually

17th AIRBORNE DIVISION
Major-General William M. Miley
HQ Company

507 Parachute Infantry Regiment (Raff)
  (attached to 82nd Airborne Division)
513 Parachute Infantry Regiment (Coutts)
193 Glider Infantry Regiment
194 Glider Infantry Regiment (Pierce)
466 Parachute Field Artillery Battalion (75mm)
680 Glider Field Artillery Battalion (75mm)
681 Glider Field Artillery Battalion (75mm)
155 Airborne Anti-Aircraft Battalion (37mm)
139 Airborne Engineer Battalion
224 Airborne Medical Company
517 Airborne Signal Company
411 Airborne Quartermaster Company
717 Airborne Ordnance Maintenance Company
Military Police Platoon

Major-General Matthew Ridgway was in England inspecting Miley's new 17th Airborne Division on 16 December, but flew back immediately to join his deputy, Jim Gavin, at XVIII (Airborne) Corps' command post in Werbomont. (U.S. Army)

getting across the Meuse had now been eliminated. The 17th was accordingly placed in the line near Neufchâteau to relieve the shattered 28th Infantry Division.

The division launched its first attack on 3 January 1945 and captured Flamierge on 7 January, but was forced out again the next day. However, the Germans began purposefully retiring on the 11th, and the village returned to the paras' control. Salle, Bertogne and Givroulle followed in quick succession and by the end of the month the division had crossed the Ourthe, occupied Steinbach and Limerle and captured Espeler

and Watermal before it was relieved by the 87th Infantry Division on the 26th. After assaulting across the river Our north of Dasburg in early February, the division was pulled out of the line back to Châlons-sur-Marne because it was needed for the assault across the Rhein in a month.

Operation 'Varsity' began on 24 March and, after the mishaps which had occurred during large-scale airborne missions earlier in the war, went off to near perfection. The 17th dropped alongside the British 6th Airborne Division north of the little town of Wesel, rapidly cleared the Schappenberg Heights, captured Diersfordt and Hamminkeln and pushed east across the river Issel. The amphibious follow-up by conventional infantry and armour was well executed and the 513th Parachute Infantry Regiment helped the British 6th Guards Armoured Brigade to capture Dorsten while the 507th overran Wulfen.

On 5 April the division was moved to the Duisburg area, assaulted across the Rhein-Herne and Berne Canals and captured Essen against only slight opposition. Two days later Major-General Miley accepted the surrender of Duisburg and for the short remainder of the war the 17th Airborne was engaged in military government duties.

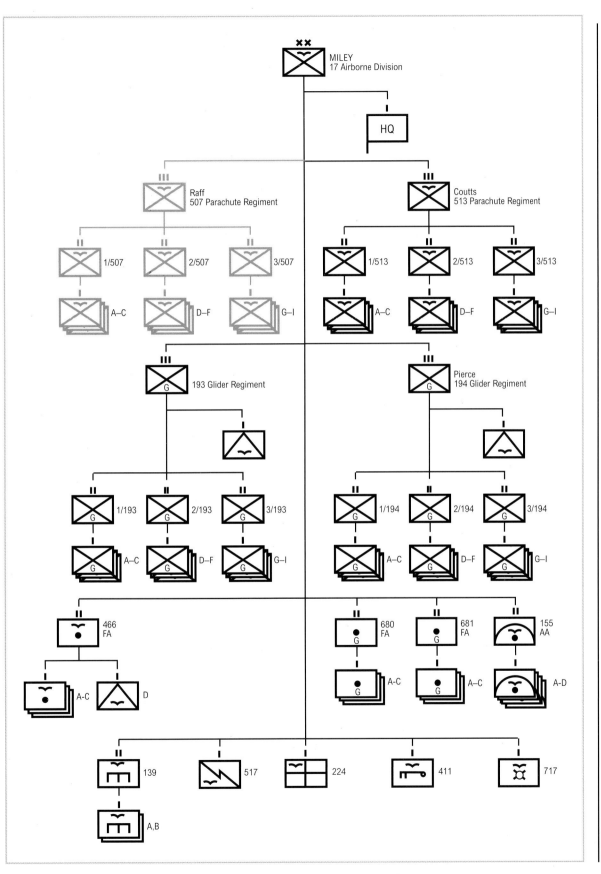

MILEY
17 Airborne Division

HQ

Raff
507 Parachute Regiment

1/507 2/507 3/507

A–C D–F G–I

Coutts
513 Parachute Regiment

1/513 2/513 3/513

A–C D–F G–I

193 Glider Regiment

Pierce
194 Glider Regiment

1/193 2/193 3/193

A–C D–F G–I

1/194 2/194 3/194

A–C D–F G–I

466
FA

A–C D

680
FA

681
FA

155
AA

A–C A–C A-D

139

517 224 411 717

A,B

101st Airborne Division

'Screaming Eagles'

The defence of Bastogne, and Brigadier-General Anthony McAuliffe's reply when called upon to surrender, have achieved the same sort of status in history as the battle of the Alamo. The parallel is, in fact, quite close, because what the outnumbered defenders did in both cases was buy time.

The 101st was unprepared for another battle so soon in December 1944. Like the 82nd 'All Americans', it had been enjoying a well-deserved respite at Reims after its arduous struggle in Holland through September and October. The two American airborne divisions constituted SHAEF's sole reserve

Brigadier-General Anthony McAuliffe was awarded the Distinguished Service Cross for his defence of Bastogne and, promoted to Major-General, given command of first the 103rd and then the 79th Infantry Divisions in 1945. (U.S. Army)

in mid-December 1944, although there were other units on their way or on standby. For that reason, Eisenhower was at first reluctant to release them until the shape and the extent of the new German offensive was better understood.

The 82nd, which was better rested and better prepared for immediate combat when Eisenhower acceded to Bradley's request to release the two divisions, headed off first. Originally destined for Bastogne, while the 101st was going to assemble at Houffalize, it was diverted to Werbomont to halt Kampfgruppe 'Peiper' in the Amblève valley. The 101st went to Bastogne in its place, arriving on 19 December. It was commanded by McAuliffe because the regular CO, Major-General Maxwell Taylor, was in Washington.

On the morning of the 19th the division arrived in an area to the west of the town bordered by the villages of Mande St-Étienne, Hemroulle and Champs. From here McAuliffe deployed the 502nd Parachute Infantry Regiment (PIR) north towards Longchamps, the

101st AIRBORNE DIVISION
Brigadier-General Anthony C. McAuliffe
pp Major-General Maxwell B. Taylor
HQ Company

502 Parachute Infantry Regiment (Chappuis)
327 Glider Infantry Regiment (Harper)
I/401 Glider Infantry Regiment (Allen)
377 Parachute Field Artillery Battalion (75mm) (Elkins)
463 Parachute Field Artillery Battalion (75mm) (Cooper)
321 Glider Field Artillery Battalion (75mm) (Carmichael)
907 Glider Field Artillery Battalion (75mm) (Nelson)
81 Airborne Anti-Aircraft Battalion (37mm) (Cox)
326 Airborne Engineer Battalion (Mozley)
326 Airborne Medical Company (Barfield)
101 Signal Company (Johnson)
426 Airborne Quartermaster Company (Horn)
801 Airborne Ordnance Maintenance Company (Patterson)
Reconnaissance Platoon
Military Police Platoon
101 Counter-Intelligence Corps Detachment
501 Parachute Infantry Regiment (Ewell) (attached)
506 Parachute Infantry Regiment (Sink) (attached)
509 Parachute Infantry Battalion (Tomasik)
  (detached to XVIII (Airborne) Corps 18 December)
CCB, 10 Armored Division (Roberts) (attached)
37 Tank Battalion, 4 Armored Division
  (attached to CCB, 10 Armored Division, 20 December)
C Company, 9 Armored Engineer Battalion,
9 Armored Division (attached)
705 Tank Destroyer Battalion (M18) (Templeton)
  (attached 20 December)
755 Field Artillery Battalion (155mm) (Hartmann) (attached)
969 Field Artillery Battalion (Colored) (155mm) (Barnes)
(attached)

506th northeast towards Foy, and the 501st directly east between Bizory and Neffe. The 327th Glider Infantry Regiment (GIR) took over the southern sector, with III/327 at Flamierge and I/327 at Senochamps, while the 326th Airborne Engineer Battalion filled in the gap between I/327 and II/327 at Marvie. Combat Command B from 10th Armored Division, which Patton had detached from XX Corps, had arrived the previous day and thrown out blocking forces at Noville, Longvilly and Wardin. The garrison was also

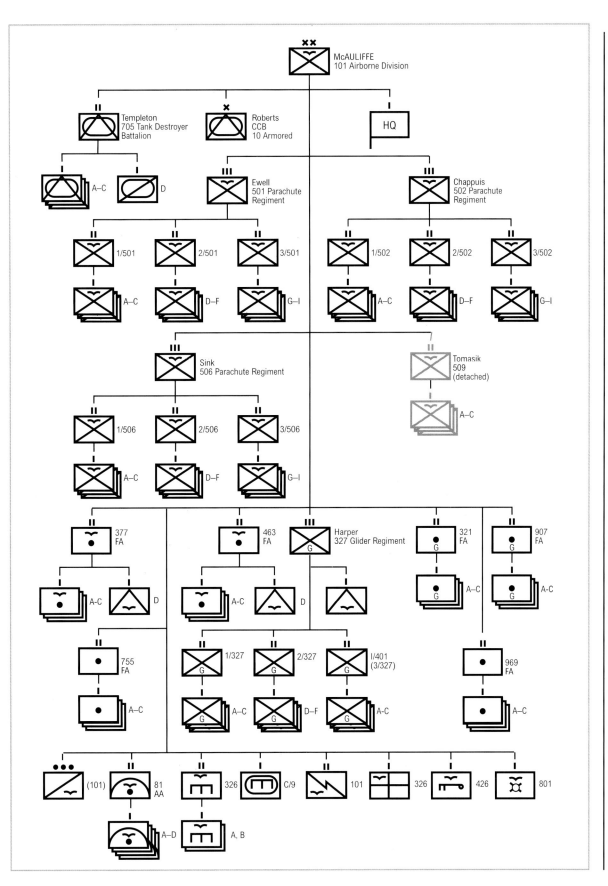

McAULIFFE
101 Airborne Division

Templeton
705 Tank Destroyer
Battalion

Roberts
CCB
10 Armored

HQ

A–C

D

Ewell
501 Parachute
Regiment

Chappuis
502 Parachute
Regiment

1/501

2/501

3/501

1/502

2/502

3/502

A–C

D–F

G–I

A–C

D–F

G–I

Sink
506 Parachute Regiment

Tomasik
509
(detached)

A–C

1/506

2/506

3/506

A–C

D–F

G–I

377
FA

463
FA

Harper
327 Glider Regiment

321
FA

907
FA

A-C

D

A–C

D

A-C

A-C

755
FA

1/327

2/327

I/401
(3/327)

969
FA

A–C

A-C

D–F

A-C

A–C

(101)

81
AA

326

C/9

101

326

426

801

A–D

A, B

Heavily festooned with bazookas, men of the 501st Parachute Infantry Regiment march out of Bastogne to an encounter with elements of Panzer Lehr at Bizory. (U.S. Army)

reinforced by surviving elements from CCR of 9th Armored Division which had been supporting the 28th Infantry Division behind 'Skyline Drive'.

These preparations complete, McAuliffe could only await events and pray for the swift arrival of Patton's III Corps. He had the equivalent of only two battalions of tanks and two armoured infantry battalions to reinforce his paras, plus one battalion of M7s with 105mm guns to support his own four field artillery battalions with their inadequate 75mm pack howitzers. Further reinforcements were essential if the vital town was to be held for more than a few days.

It was an unusual situation for the men of the 101st Airborne who were more used to attacking than defending, and to being dropped from the air rather than carried in trucks, but morale was high. Although less combat experienced than the 82nd, the 'Screaming Eagles' had already played a decisive role in influencing the outcome of the war in France and Holland.

The second U.S. airborne division to be created, the 101st had been activated at Camp Claiborne, Louisiana, on 15 August 1942 and moved to join the 82nd at Fort Bragg, North Carolina, a month later. Its first commander, until Maxwell Taylor took over in March 1944, was Major-General William Lee, who shipped the division to England in September 1943, destination Normandy.

On 6 June 1944 the 101st was dropped before daylight, alongside the 82nd, in a broad triangle inland from 'Utah' beach, the objective being to secure the right flank of the Allied front while the British 6th Airborne similarly secured the left. The 502nd PIR quickly seized the beach exits at St-Martin-de-Vareville and Pouppeville, but the 501st, landing around St-Côme-du-Mont, quickly ran into problems with 6 Fallschirm Regiment outside Carentan. Even reinforced by the 502nd PIR and the 327th GIR, it took until the 11th to force the defenders out. The division then assumed a defensive posture and repelled counter-attacks until relieved by the 83rd Infantry Division on the 27th. It then returned to England.

The 101st's next operation took place unexpectedly in September, after Montgomery conceived the audacious plan to seize a crossing over the Rhein at Arnhem by laying an 'airborne carpet' across Holland for the tanks of XXX Corps. The division dropped around Eindhoven on 17 September and captured the bridge at Veghel, but failed to take the bridges intact over the Wilhelmina Canal at Best and Son. Although the British Guards Armoured Division managed to get through Eindhoven and up to Nijmegen, seized by the 82nd, they failed to get to Arnhem in time to secure the 'bridge too far' captured by the British 1st Airborne Division.

After fighting off counter-attacks in Holland during October and November, the division was sent to Reims to recuperate before being sent to Bastogne in December. After the 'Battle of the Bulge' it saw no further real action but enjoyed the distinction of reaching Berchtesgaden on 7 May 1945.

Combat Command B, 10th Armored Division

The 10th Armored Division was moved from Merzig on the river Saare to Luxembourg on 17 December and William Roberts' CCB reached Bastogne the following day. Under orders to protect the eastern approaches until the arrival of the 101st Airborne next day, Roberts assigned each of his tank and infantry battalion commanders a village to

Colonel William Roberts' skilful deployment of the limited forces at his disposal played a significant part in denying Bastogne to the Germans until help arrived. (U.S. Signal Corps)

defend, reinforcing them with parts of 9th Armored's CCR as they trickled west. Although one by one driven back into the main Bastogne perimeter, Roberts' battalions accomplished their task with distinction.

The division had landed in France only in September and CCB's first battle had been at Merzig

as part of Patton's XX Corps. Back with its parent corps in February 1945, CCB crossed the Saar under heavy fire, captured a bridge intact across the Mosel at the beginning of March and crossed the Rhein at the end of the month. It ended the war on the Danube at Innsbruck.

COMBAT COMMAND B, 10th ARMORED DIVISION
Colonel William L. Roberts
HQ Company

---

3 Tank Battalion (Cherry)
C Company, 21 Tank Battalion (Devereaux)
20 Armored Infantry Battalion (Desobry)
54 Armored Infantry Battalion (O'Hara)
420 Armored Field Artillery Battalion (M7) (Browne)
C Company, 55 Armored Engineer Battalion
B Battery, 796 Anti-Aircraft Battalion (M15/M16)
C Company, 609 Tank Destroyer Battalion (M18)
D Troop, 90 Cavalry Reconnaissance Squadron, Mechanized (M5)
37 Tank Battalion, 4 Armored Division (attached)
C Company, 9 Armored Engineer Battalion, 9 Armored Division (attached)

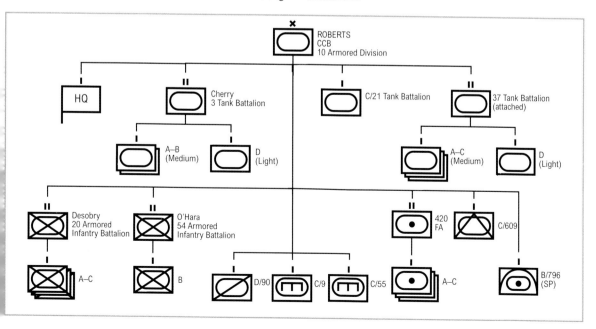

U.S. VIII CORPS' BATTLES

106th Infantry Division

Schnee Eifel – December 16–19

What went wrong? Given that the three infantry regiments of Major-General Alan Jones' 106th Division were thinly spread, their positions were nothing like the skirmish line held by the 28th to their south. They occupied well dug-in field fortifications with felled trees and shovelled earth protection against artillery and mortar fire – prepared over the previous month by the 2nd Infantry Division, which had vacated its relatively comfortable billet for the attack towards the Rur and Urft dams. The 106th was fresh, having arrived on the Continent only 10 days earlier; and its opponents were predominantly equally 'green' troops from a rehabilitated Luftwaffe field division, the 18th. Yet, when the assault began on 16 December, the 106th failed to respond to the challenge. The division's records are incomplete, for obvious reasons, and survivors' accounts are full of accusations of other people's incompetence, but what actually happened was very simple.

The German 18 Volksgrenadier Division's 294 Grenadier Regiment exploited the vacuum in the appropriately named Losheim Gap caused by the precipitate withdrawal of the covering 14th Cavalry Group. Sweeping through Roth and capturing Auw, it debouched on to the flank and rear of Colonel George Deschenaux's 422nd Regiment on the 106th's left flank. Simultaneously, the German 293 Grenadier Regiment exploited the thinly held boundary between the lines of Colonel Charles Cavender's 423rd Regiment in the centre, and Colonel Alexander Reid's 424th on the right flank.

While Reid's regiment was able to fall back through Winterspelt to join CCB of 9th Armored Division on the southeastern shoulder of the St Vith horseshoe, there was no salvation for the 106th's other two regiments. The division's indecisive CO, Alan Jones, delayed using CCB in a counter-attack because he had been promised the support of the entire 7th Armored Division as well. Unsurprisingly, given the distance, the weather and the roads, this did not begin

Survivors from the 106th: Sergeant Slashy and Private Phillips of the 424th Infantry Regiment, which escaped envelopment, roll up their sleeping bags, weariness and disappointment written on their faces.

(U.S. Army)

16/12/1944	17/12	18/12	19/12	20/12	21/12	22/12	23/12	24/12	25/12	26/12	27/12	28/12	29/12
pages 68-72	77-78	73-76	79-82,85-86	27-34,83-84	87-88,94-95	39-40		35-38,89-90					

deploying until late on 17 December, and by the 18th a counter-attack was no longer feasible.

On the 106th's left flank, the Volksgrenadiers began by trying to take out the division's artillery, but a counter-attack by the reserve II/423rd stopped them; while in the centre, the village of Bleialf, which had been briefly captured, was retaken by B Company of the 81st Engineer Combat Battalion. Both small victories were shortlived. On 17 December 294 Grenadier Regiment captured Schönberg and its bridge over the river Our, blocking the two American regiments' line of retreat towards St Vith. At around the same time, 293 Grenadier Regiment recaptured Bleialf

Deschenaux's 422nd and Cavender's 423rd Infantry Regiments were trapped by 18 Volksgrenadier Division's bold pincer attack which captured Bleialf and Schönberg behind them. They waited in vain for the promised counter-attack by 7th Armored.

and also started heading for Schönberg. The jaws had closed, the trap was complete and, lacking firm direction from Alan Jones, the 422nd and 423rd, in effect, did nothing. Only the 424th in the south continued its fighting withdrawal towards the Our.

Alan Jones finally, at about 0730 hrs on 18 December, ordered the two trapped regiments to attempt a southwesterly retreat. Only Cavender still had radio contact, so he had to pass the word to Deschenaux by hand. As the two columns were approaching Bleialf at about midday, Jones countermanded his earlier order and sent them backtracking towards Schönberg. The last message they got from him, just before midnight, was an order to recapture Schönberg! Although the men still had spirit, it was 'mission impossible' because they had virtually no ammunition left. At about 1600 hrs on 19 December, after ordering their men to disable their weapons, Cavender and Deschenaux ordered surrender.

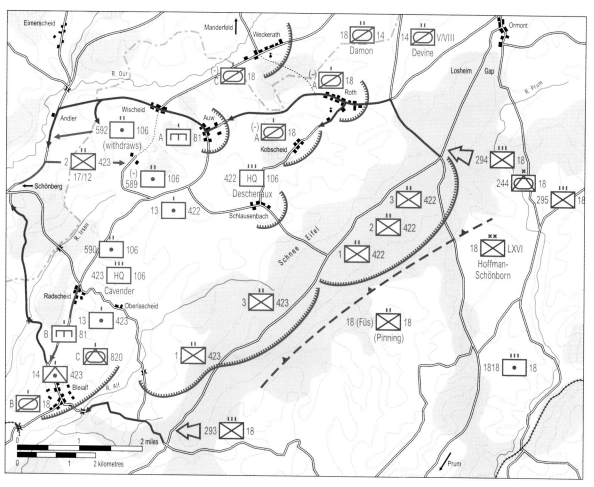

16/12/1944	17/12	18/12	19/12	20/12	21/12	22/12	23/12	24/12	25/12	26/12	27/12	28/12	29/12
pages 68-72	77-78	73-76	79-82,85-86	27-34,83-84	87-88,94-95	39-40		35-38,89-90					

U.S. VIII CORPS' BATTLES
112th Infantry Regiment, 28th Infantry Division

Sevenig/Ouren – December 16–18

The German LVIII Korps' attack on 16 December drove a wedge between Colonel Gustin Nelson's 112th and Colonel Hurley Fuller's 110th Regiments, and for the next four days Nelson fought a private war more or less completely out of touch with the 28th Infantry Division's CO, Major-General Norman Cota. Nelson's regiment, badly mauled in the Hürtgen Forest but now back up to strength, occupied a six-mile (10-km) stretch of front between Lützkampen, where it abutted on to the 424th Regiment of 106th Infantry Division, and Kalborn on the left flank of the 110th. Roughly in the centre of its line, III/112th occupied a small salient east of the river Our into Germany itself at Sevenig. From here, sentries had heard enemy troop movements over the preceding two nights, but nothing which appeared untoward. In fact, it was 116 Panzer and 560 Volksgrenadier Divisions moving into their attack positions.

At 0530 hrs the men of Major Walden Woodward's III/112th were woken by the sound of heavy artillery fire to their north and south, but nothing seemed to be happening in their own sector. This was deliberate on the part of the German Korps' commander, General Krüger, who was banking on surprise to get his men across the Our. Thus, the first Woodward's men knew of the attack was when the false dawn revealed the shadowy shapes of German infantrymen almost on top of their lines. They were the assault companies of 1130 Volksgrenadier Regiment. Simultaneously, 60 and 156 Panzergrenadier Regiments attacked Lieutenant-Colonel William Allen's I/112th on Woodward's left.

The German assault companies at Sevenig broke into the 3rd Battalion's lines but then faltered under heavy fire from the 229th Field Artillery Battalion and were thrown out when Nelson launched two companies of Lieutenant-Colonel J.L. MacSalka's reserve 2nd Battalion in a counter-attack. In the north, the assault company of 60 Panzergrenadier Regiment came under enfilading fire from the 424th Regiment and went to ground, while 156 Panzergrenadier Regiment broke through to the 112th's artillery

Before the assault: men of Colonel Gustin Nelson's 112th Infantry Regiment's headquarters company carefully fuse anti-tank mines. This took great care with fingers half numbed by the cold.
(Imperial War Museum)

16/12/1944		17/12	18/12		19/12	20/12		21/12		22/12	23/12	24/12	25/12	26/12	27/12	28/12	29/12
pages 66-67,70-72		77-78	73-76		79-82,85-86	27-34,83-84		87-88,94-95		39-40		35-38,89-90					

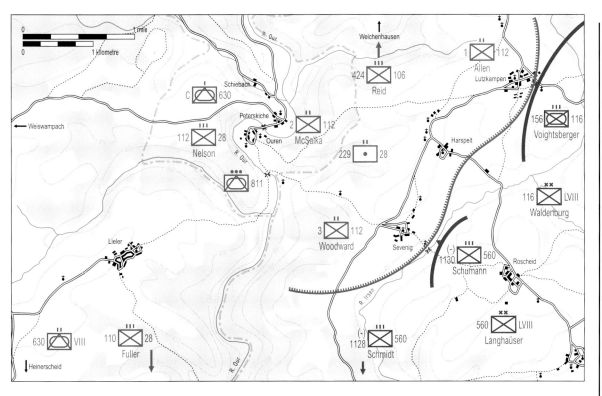

Although the German grenadiers broke through the 112th Infantry Regiment's lines and eventually forced them to fall back behind the Our, they then found the Ouren bridge would not bear the weight of their tanks.

positions at Welchenhausen but was repulsed by the quad .50 machine-guns on the supporting M16 half-tracks. The first round had gone to the 112th, but the Germans had a sally port at Lützkampen and 1128 Volksgrenadier Regiment to the south had severed communications with the 110th Regiment at Heinerscheid.

With German tanks now in Lützkampen, Colonel Nelson deployed the towed 76mm guns of C Company, 630th Tank Destroyer Battalion, west of the Our overlooking Ouren, reinforced by four M18s from 9th Armored Division's 811th Tank Destroyer Battalion. It was none too soon because, about an hour before dawn on 17 December, German artillery began pounding at the 229th Field Artillery Battalion's positions, while a full company of Panthers began rolling towards the bridge at Ouren.

Companies A and D of Allen's I/112th were overrun and by 0930 hrs German tanks were overlooking Nelson's command post in Ouren. The 811th's M18s had accounted for four Panthers, and the anti-tank guns on the west bank of the Our now accounted for four more. A counter-attack by II/112th could only slow, not halt, the German build-up, and at 1400 hrs Colonel Nelson had to order the 229th Field Artillery Battalion to redeploy west of the river.

III/112th, which had not been attacked by tanks, was still holding on by the skin of its teeth, helped by the Germans' own West Wall pillboxes. I/112th, however, was in a precarious position following the withdrawal of the 424th on its northern flank, and the Germans' steady advance. After a messenger finally got through to General Cota mid-afternoon on the 17th, Nelson received permission to fall back behind the Our. III/112th circled south and west and rejoined the rest of the regiment around Weiswampach, while the remnants of I/112th marched straight through Ouren under cover of darkness, while an officer shouted commands in German!

The regiment had a respite during the 18th because Krüger had redirected 116 Panzer Division to exploit the hole in 110th Infantry Regiment's lines further south. On the 19th, however, Nelson had no option but to fall back further through Beiler and thence to join the defenders in front of St Vith.

16/12/1944	17/12	18/12	19/12	20/12	21/12	22/12	23/12	24/12	25/12	26/12	27/12	28/12	29/12
pages 66-67,70-72	77-78	73-76	79-82,85-86	27-34,83-84	87-88,94-95	39-40		35-38,89-90					

U.S. VIII CORPS' BATTLES
I/110th Infantry Regiment, 28th Infantry Division

Marnach/Clervaux – December 16–18

Château Clervaux has a convincing ring to it as the name on the label of a decent bottle of vin rouge, but the only 'rouge' on the flagstones of the 12th-century castle in the centre of Clervaux on the morning of 18 December 1944 was the blood red of the victims of the battle which had almost consumed the ancient crenellated fortress.

The little town of Clervaux, nestling in the valley of the river Clerf just a couple of miles (3 km) east of the German border at Dasburg, became central to Colonel Hurley Fuller's defence of the 10-mile (16-km) front allocated to the 110th Regiment of the 28th Infantry Division. However, he had only two battalions in the line because Lieutenant-Colonel Ross Henbest's 2nd was in divisional reserve halfway back to Bastogne at Donnange. Lieutenant-Colonel Donald Paul's I/110th thus held the northern sector from Heinerscheid via Marnach to Hosingen, where Major Harold Milton's III/110th continued the line south to Weiler. Beyond that, the division's 109th Regiment took over, although this would be hit not by Fifth Panzer but by Seventh Armee.

Because two infantry battalions could not possibly hold such a stretch of front in any depth, Colonel Fuller had constructed a form of 'hedgehog' line using the villages along the ridge which bisects the rivers Our and Clerf (known to the Americans as 'Skyline Drive') as strongpoints. Company A was furthest north, abutting the right flank of the 112th Regiment at Heinerscheid. Company B and a platoon from the 630th Tank Destroyer Battalion held the centre at Marnach, with Colonel Fuller's regimental command post a mile behind at Clervaux; while Company C was a little to the southwest at Munshausen.

Opposing Donald Paul's 1st Battalion on the east bank of the Our behind Dasburg was the whole of 2 Panzer Division and a substantial part of 26 Volksgrenadier Division, but despite the disparity in strength they would not find the battle a walkover. Their attack began before the artillery barrage opened up at 0530 hrs on 16 December, with German assault companies infiltrating the woods on the west bank of the Our while it was still pitch dark. The first inkling Colonel Fuller had that Germans were already across the river was a radio message from Harold Milton's III/110th at about 0615 hrs saying that enemy troops were already at Holzthum. Fuller immediately notified General Cota at the divisional headquarters in Wiltz.

The assault against the 1st Battalion led by 28 Panzer Pionier Abteilung and II/304 Panzergrenadier Regiment was delayed by a minefield, but by 0800 hrs they were up to the well dug-in men of Company B at Marnach. Here, they were hotly received but rapidly infiltrated the woods north and south of the village, so Colonel Paul ordered Companies A and C to counter-attack their flanks north and south from Heinerscheid and Munshausen. Both the relieving forces ran into heavy fire and could make only slow headway.

Meanwhile – it was now about 1000 hrs – General Cota had not been idle despite the very limited resources available to him. Notwithstanding Fuller's pleas, he refused to release the reserve II/110th, but did order Companies A and B of the 707th Tank Battalion to the regiment's aid. Company A, leaving a platoon in Munshausen, moved out towards Marnach in the wake of Company C's infantry, while Company B went to the aid of the 3rd Battalion. For the time

Lieutenant-Colonel Donald Paul's isolated companies on 'Skyline Drive' suffered heavily in trying to deny 2 Panzer Division westward access across the river Clerf, but their defence at Marnach and Clervaux delayed the Germans long enough for Bastogne to be reinforced.

16/12/1944	17/12	18/12	19/12	20/12	21/12	22/12	23/12	24/12	25/12	26/12	27/12	28/12	29/12
pages 66-69	77-78	73-76	79-82,85-86	27-34,83-84	87-88,94-95	39-40		35-38,89-90					

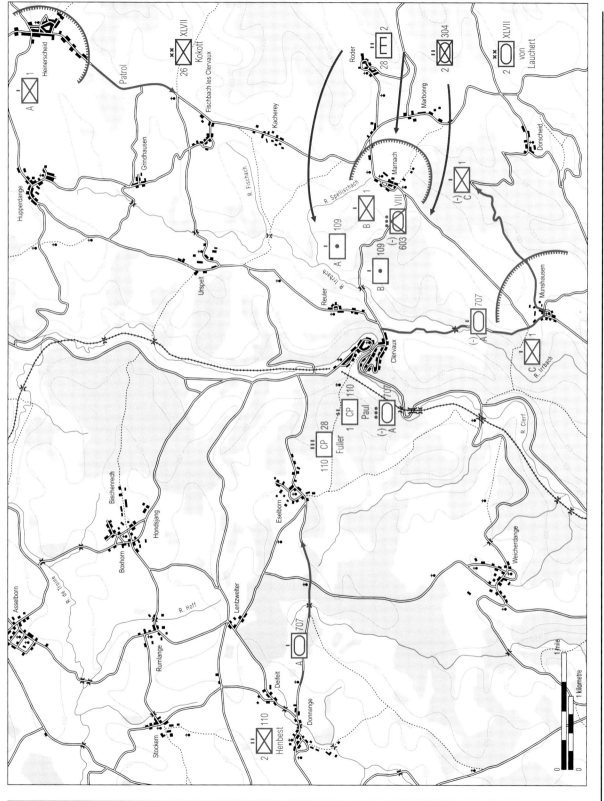

Heinerscheid

A 1

Patrol

26 Kokott XLVII

Fischbach les Clervaux

Grindhausen

Hupperdange

Kacherey

R. Fischach

R. Spellischach

Roder

28 2 E

Marbonng

2 304

2 von Lauchert XLVII

Dorscheid

Marnach

(-) C 1

Urspelt

Reuler

R. Irrbach

B 1

A 109

B 109

VIII

(-) 603

Munshausen

707 (-) A

C 1 R. Irrbach

Clervaux

Bischenech

Hondsjang

Boxhorn

Asselborn

R. de Tretne

R. Hoff

Eselborn

Lentzweiler

1 CP 110

CP Paul

(-) A 707

28 CP Fuller

110

R. Clerf

Weicherdange

Rumlange

Stockem

Deifelt

Donange

707 (-) A

2 110 Henbest

1 mile

1 kilometre

16/12/1944	17/12	18/12	19/12	20/12	21/12	22/12	23/12	24/12	25/12	26/12	27/12	28/12	29/12
pages 66-69	77-78	73-76	79-82,85-86	27-34,83-84	87-88,94-95	39-40		35-38,89-90					

71

After the battle, the little town of Clervaux lies in ruins. The château defended by Captain Claude Mackey's headquarters company of the 110th is to the right of the twin-spired church. (U.S. Signal Corps)

being, though, the struggle remained an infantry one, because German engineers were still struggling to erect the 60-ton bridge at Dasburg so that 2 Panzer Division's tanks could advance.

Of A/707th's platoons of M4s, one caught up with the Company C infantry and returned with them to Munshausen because of the plight of III/110th to the south. One platoon remained in Clervaux while the third pressed on to Marnach. Radio contact was lost at dusk. Company B had finally been overrun, as had Battery A of the 109th Field Artillery Battalion which had been supporting them. Battery B, protected by a scratch 'Company D' which Fuller assembled from men who had been on leave in Clervaux, continued firing. By this time, however, the German engineers had completed the bridge over the Our and 2 Panzer Division's tanks were on the march.

Still believing that some hope existed for Company B in Marnach, early on the morning of 17 December Colonel Fuller launched a three-pronged attack towards the village. From Heinerscheid, the 707th Tank Battalion's light company of M5s headed south at about 0700 hrs; within 10 minutes they had lost 11 tanks, which ended that sortie. General Cota had also agreed to release the reserve II/110th at long last, less one company which was ordered to Wiltz. Attacking east from Clervaux, the remaining two

companies ran straight into the arms of 2 Panzer Division and were stopped dead in their tracks. The third sortie, by the platoon of M4s still in Munshausen, reached Marnach only to find no one left alive. The battle for Clervaux itself was about to begin.

Although the tanks of 3 Panzer Regiment could approach only along the narrow road winding tortuously down towards the river Clerf, they soon overcame the one remaining platoon of the 707th Tank Battalion which advanced to meet them, and German infantry were quickly into the southeastern parts of Clervaux. Further help for the 110th arrived at about midday: the 19 M4s of Company B of the 2nd Tank Battalion from 9th Armored Division's CCR. Again, however, their effectiveness was dissipated by sending one troop to Heinerscheid and one to Reuler. By late afternoon the companies in both villages had been overrun. At 1825 hrs Colonel Fuller reported that he was evacuating Clervaux, whose streets were now full of German tanks and grenadiers. Only minutes later, he was captured. The final round went to the little garrison of headquarters troops acommanded by Captain Claude Mackey still in the château. While one GI played a piano, according to a Belgian refugee sheltering in the fortress, snipers fired through the ancient arrow slits, and a solitary M4 in the courtyard exchanged fire with the approaching Panthers until a return shot blew its turret off. The last bastion of I/110th held out until noon on 18 December but, with flames consuming half the castle, when a German tank finally blasted its way into the courtyard and began firing at close quarters, Mackey had no option other than to raise a white flag.

16/12/1944	17/12	18/12	19/12	20/12	21/12	22/12	23/12	24/12	25/12	26/12	27/12	28/12	29/12
pages 66-69	77-78	73-76	79-82,85-86	27-34,83-84	87-88,94-95	39-40		35-38,89-90					

U.S. VIII CORPS' BATTLES
44th Engineer Combat Battalion

Wiltz – December 18–19

By midday on 18 December it was clear to both Major-General Norman Cota and to VIII Corps' commander, Troy Middleton, that the 28th Infantry Division's remaining positions east of the river Clerf were untenable, and any thought of counter-attack with the meagre forces available was out of the question.

On the north of the division's front, the 112th Regiment was falling back in line with the 424th towards 9th Armored Division's CCB at St Vith. In the centre, the 110th Regiment had evaporated as a fighting force apart from elements of the 3rd Battalion which were gradually giving ground back through Consthum. In the south, the 109th Regiment was in a similar position to the 112th, out of contact and retiring towards the lines of 9th Armored Division's CCA, while the remnants of CCR were urgently needed at Bastogne.

In the light of the rapidly deteriorating situation on the afternoon of 18 December, General Cota decided to remove his headquarters back to Sibret, southwest of Bastogne. Before he left, Cota organised a scratch defence for Wiltz comprising men from the headquarters and quartermaster companies, bandsmen and stragglers. The latter included half a dozen M4s from the 707th Tank Battalion; a few M18s and towed guns from the 630th Tank Destroyer Battalion; some M15s and M8s from the 447th Anti-Aircraft Battalion and 28th Reconnaissance Troops; plus a couple of understrength batteries of the 687th Field Artillery Battalion's 105mm howitzers from VIII Corps' reserve. Overall command was vested in Cota's executive officer, Colonel Dan Strickler.

The mainstay of the defence, however, was Lieutenant-Colonel Clarion Kjeldseth's 600-strong 44th Engineer Combat Battalion, also from corps reserve. Two companies set up blocking positions in the hamlets of Eschweiler and Erpeldange, right in the path of Panzer Lehr, while the third remained in Wiltz. The irony of the whole situation is that, if Middleton

Despite the small number of troops engaged, the street fighting in Wiltz was intense, with troops on both sides taking advantage of stone walls for cover. Note the fortunate GI in the foreground carries a Thompson M1A1, a simplified version of the famous M1928 with straight foregrip and box magazine.
(Imperial War Museum)

16/12/1944	17/12	18/12	19/12	20/12	21/12	22/12	23/12	24/12	25/12	26/12	27/12	28/12	29/12
pages 66-72	77-78	75-76	79-82,85-86	27-34,83-84	87-88,94-95	39-40		35-38,89-90					

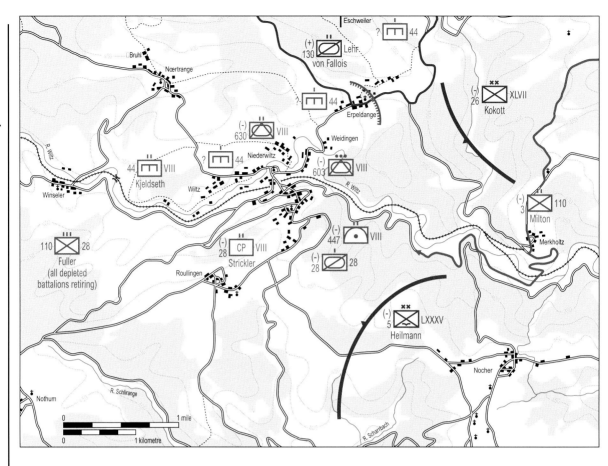

Wiltz was not a prime objective to the Germans and its defence, unlike that at Clervaux, Hosingen, Consthum and Holzthum, did not delay them.

had not ordered that Wiltz be defended, it would not have been attacked because it lay south of Panzer Lehr's Rollbahn. However, because the garrison posed a threat to the German flank, it could not be ignored.

Having driven the 200-odd survivors of Major Harold Milton's III/110th southwest out of Consthum to Nocher, Panzer Lehr's Aufklärungs Abteilung turned left at the road junction east of Eschweiler and headed for Wiltz, while 902 Panzergrenadier Division, accompanied personally by Generalleutnant Fritz Bayerlein, headed west through Eschweiler. They quickly disposed of four M18s supporting the company of engineers in the village, but Kjeldseth's men held their fire until the German tanks had passed, then opened up on the infantry. The Panzergrenadiers rallied quickly, however, and by dusk had driven the outnumbered

engineers back to Weidingen. The German recce battalion did not attack but rejoined the rest of Panzer Lehr, leaving infantry of the 26th Volksgrenadier Division to keep the defenders of Wiltz pinned down.

Early on the morning of 19 December the sadly depleted III/110th trudged from the southeast to swell the garrison, but it was hotly followed by paratroops from 5 Fallschirm Division. Then, mid-afternoon, infantry and assault guns from 26 Volksgrenadier Division also attacked from the northeast, driving the engineers in Erpeldange back across the river Wiltz into the town. Kjeldseth's battalion had already lost over 25 per cent of its original strength and, by the time night fell, the American perimeter was as full of holes as Swiss cheese. Colonel Strickler ordered all his men to fall back as best they could towards Sibret and Bastogne, but the countryside in between was swarming with Germans by this time and the precious few who made it safely were cold, wet, starving and exhausted. It was a big price to pay for a little town the Germans did not want in the first place.

16/12/1944	17/12	18/12	19/12	20/12	21/12	22/12	23/12	24/12	25/12	26/12	27/12	28/12	29/12
pages 66-72	77-78	75-76	79-82,85-86	27-34,83-84	87-88,94-95	39-40		35-38,89-90					

U.S. VIII CORPS' BATTLES

CCA, 9th Armored Division

Ermsdorf/Savelborn – December 18–20

On 18 December, after two days of reverses with only minor local successes, Combat Command A had straightened its lines some 3 miles (5 km) east of the river Sauer and was preparing to counter-attack. Unfortunately, the opposing 276 Volksgrenadier Division had the same idea and, in effect, Colonel Thomas Harrold's men ran into a nasty ambush.

At the beginning of the German offensive on the 16th, CCA occupied a 3-mile (5-km) front linking and supporting 4th Infantry Division on its right and the 109th Regiment of 28th Infantry Division on its left. Its most forward element was Lieutenant-Colonel Kenneth Collins' 60th Armored Infantry Battalion just east of Beaufort, around Dillingen, overlooking the

Engineers moving damaged 9th Armored Division M4s to a field workshop. A surprising number of tanks abandoned on battlefields could be repaired within a few hours. (U.S. Army)

Sauer. The Volksgrenadiers' main assault across the river took place north and south, through Wallendorf and Bollendorf, encircling three companies of Collins' men and forcing him to withdraw the remainder to Beaufort, which also had to be abandoned shortly after dark on the 17th.

By the 18th, however, Colonel Harrold felt more secure, having brought forward his own 19th Tank Battalion to reinforce the 3rd Armored Field Artillery Battalion, Battery A of the 482nd Anti-Aircraft Battalion and Troops A and B of the 89th Cavalry Reconnaissance Squadron which, with Collins' 60th Infantry, constituted the main 'teeth' of the command. In addition, Harrold had the M18s of the attached 811th Tank Destroyer Battalion's Company B.

On 18 December, therefore, feeling secure that there was no more danger of being outflanked, Colonel Harrold prepared to counter-attack the 276th Volksgrenadiers, whose commander, Generalleutnant Kurt Möhring, had actually been killed

16/12/1944		17/12	18/12	19/12	20/12	21/12		22/12	23/12	24/12	25/12	26/12	27/12	28/12	29/12
pages 66-72		77-78	73-74	79-82,85-86	27-34,83-84	87-88,94-95		39-40		35-38,89-90					

the previous evening while preparing his own latest assault. He had assembled a battalion of grenadiers and an anti-tank company (with no fewer than 54 Panzerfausts) in the woods east of the Ermsdorf–Savelborn road with the intention of striking towards Medernach.

Colonel Harrold's intention was to rescue the three 60th Armored Infantry companies northeast of Beaufort. He assembled what small reserve he had – one company of M4s, a platoon of M5s, a cavalry platoon, the intelligence and reconnaissance platoon and a company of combat engineers – and formed them into two task forces. The leading one, under Captain John Hall, was preceded by the I&R platoon, which set off before dawn along the narrow track leading to Berens through the woods where the Volksgrenadiers were assembled. It was wiped out

The German 276 Volksgrenadier Division enjoyed a very shortlived victory over CCA/9th Armored east of Medernach on 18 December and its later attack toward Christnach was a disaster.

almost to a man by wicked crossfire from both sides. Hall's main force, following the same path after daybreak, was led by the light tanks. The first M5 was hit by a Panzerfaust round, blocking the road, and the second task force under Major Tommie Philbeck arrived in the middle of a firefight. After six more tanks had been destroyed, both groups retired to Savelborn.

That the Germans did not pursue their advantage is due to the fact that the Volksgrenadiers' new CO, Oberst Hugo Dempwolff, wanted to take stock. He spent 19 December reorganising his forces for a new attack towards Christnach, which gave about half the men of the three surrounded companies of the 60th Armored Infantry a chance to rejoin their battalion. By the evening of the 19th, Dempwolff had actually received four of the precious StuG assault guns assigned to Seventh Armee. Using his one uncommitted regiment, the 987th, he attacked towards Christnach next afternoon, but by this time CCA's artillery and tank destroyers were well dug-in and the attack failed. Smoke from the burning StuGs marked the high tide level of what turned out to be 276 Volksgrenadier Division's last assault.

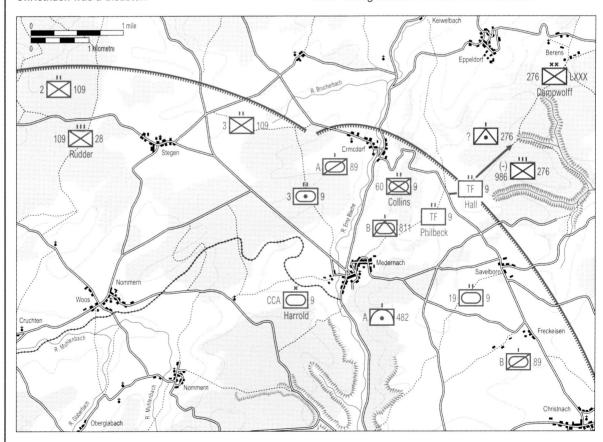

	16/12/1944	17/12	18/12	19/12	20/12	21/12	22/12	23/12	24/12	25/12	26/12	27/12	28/12	29/12
	pages 66-72	77-78	73-74	79-82,85-86	27-34,83-84	87-88,94-95	39-40		35-38,89-90					

U.S. VIII CORPS' BATTLES

CCR, 9th Armored Division and Team 'Cherry'

Longvilly/Mageret – December 17–19

D uring 18 December the defences around Bastogne were gradually beginning to take shape, although they were still full of holes. There was, as yet, no cohesive line except for a weak eastern perimeter established by Lieutenant-Colonel Sam Tabets' 158th Engineer Combat Battalion running from Foy through Bizory to Neffe. What General Middleton had arranged before he departed for his new corps headquarters at Neufchâteau on the 19th was a series of delaying actions in the villages north, east and south of Bastogne to give the

Even though they suffered grievous losses, CCR/9th Armored's roadblock teams did delay 2 Panzer Division's westward advance and forced it to veer northwest of Bastogne at a time when the town itself lay wide open.

101st Airborne Division time to deploy.

He had, in fact, already begun putting this process into action a day earlier by assigning those elements of Colonel Joseph Gilbreth's CCR, 9th Armored Division, which were not already engaged in immediate support of the 28th Infantry Division, to block the roads from Clervaux and Wiltz. A task force under Captain Lawrence Rose, comprising his own Company A of the 2nd Tank Battalion plus a company from Lieutenant-Colonel Robert Booth's 52nd Armored Infantry Battalion and a platoon of engineers, was placed at the Antoniushof farm road junction just north of Lullange. A second task force, comprising Company C of Lieutenant-Colonel Ralph Harper's 2nd Tank Battalion and another company of armoured infantry, established itself further back at Baraque d'Allerborn. Already there they found about

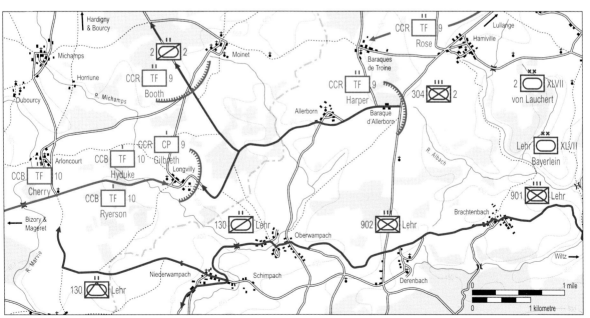

16/12/1944	17/12	18/12	19/12	20/12	21/12	22/12	23/12	24/12	25/12	26/12	27/12	28/12	29/12
pages 66-72		73-76	79-82,85-86	27-34,83-84	87-88,94-95	39-40		35-38,89-90					

77

Photographed in January 1945 during the Allied counter-offensive, the road between Longvilly and Mageret was still strewn with abandoned M4s and wrecked trucks from CCR of 9th and CCB of 10th Armored Divisions. (U.S. Army)

100 stragglers from the 28th Infantry Division's 110th Regiment which had been rallied by a divisional staff officer, Colonel Theodore Seely. Behind these two task forces, at Longvilly itself, Gilbreth set up his headquarters and put Colonel Booth, with his third infantry company and the remainder of CCR (including most of the 73rd Armored Field Artillery Battalion's M7s) on the ridge to the north.

Task Force 'Rose' did not survive long. By mid-morning on the 18th the reconnaissance battalion of 2 Panzer Division which had broken through at Clervaux had reached the road junction. By 1400 hrs it was reinforced by a company of 3 Panzer Regiment PzKpfw IVs, and within half an hour Rose had lost seven M4s. The remaining five broke out after dark towards Houffalize but were ambushed and only a handful of men made it back to Bastogne. At about the same time, Task Force 'Harper' at Baraque d'Allerborn came under attack. Two of Company C's platoons of Shermans were wiped out and the supporting com-pany of infantry lost heavily to machine-gun fire. Harper himself was killed and the survivors trudged back to Longvilly. Task Force 'Booth' fared no better. Although it was not attacked during the night of the 18th/19th, German tanks got behind it through Bourcy. Booth had lost communications with Gilbreth and decided to pull back northwest to avoid encirclement. However, he was ambushed near Hardigny and only 225 of his men eventually made it back to Bastogne.

At Longvilly itself, welcome reinforcements arrived during the evening of the 18th. Colonel William Roberts' CCB of Patton's 10th Armored Division had begun deploying at Bastogne during the day and was split into three main task forces, 'Cherry', 'Desobry' and 'O'Hara'. That commanded by Lieutenant-Colonel Henry Cherry, CO of the 3rd Tank Battalion, established its headquarters in Neffe. From here he despatched an advance guard under 1st Lieutenant Edward Hyduke towards Longvilly. This encountered a scene of indescribable confusion with men and vehicles streaming back towards Mageret, and Hyduke threw out his four M4s and five M5s as a screen. Behind him the main task force, Captain William Ryerson's Company A of the 3rd Tank Battalion, deployed defensively, under orders not to venture further east than Longvilly.

German troops from Panzer Lehr occupied Mageret during the night of the 18th/19th and Colonels Cherry and Gilbreth ordered their forces to fight their way through back to Bastogne, leaving Hyduke's advance guard as a rearguard. This resulted in a massive traffic jam on the narrow road, and there were so many Germans now in Mageret that a breakthrough was impossible. Led by Ryerson, however, the bulk of Team 'Cherry' managed to fight its way cross-country to relative safety at Bizory, which was now occupied by men of the 101st Airborne Division's 501st Parachute Infantry Regiment.

16/12/1944	17/12	18/12	19/12	20/12	21/12	22/12	23/12	24/12	25/12	26/12	27/12	28/12	29/12
pages 66-72		73-76	79-82,85-86	27-34,83-84	87-88,94-95	39-40		35-38,89-90					

U.S. VIII CORPS' BATTLES

501st Parachute Infantry Regiment, 101st Airborne Division

Neffe/Bizory – December 19–20

About an hour after the weak winter sun had lightened the clouds overhanging Bastogne on the morning of 20 December, the men of Major Sammie Homan's 2nd Battalion, 501st Parachute Infantry Regiment (II/501st PIR), welcomed into their ranks the nine M4s (some sources say seven) and other battered, weary but still confident survivors of Captain William Ryerson's task force from Team 'Cherry'. Forty-eight hours earlier the paras had been resting at Camp Mourmelon, outside Reims, France. Now, after an eight-hour, 107-mile (170-km) journey by truck through rain, sleet and snow, II/501st was deployed on the left flank of Lieutenant-Colonel Julian Ewell's regiment east of Bastogne. The 501st was the first of the 101st Airborne Division's four regiments to reach the town, at around midnight on 18 December. By this time the battle for the roadblocks east of the town was in full swing, and there was a grave danger that a determined German armoured thrust could seize Bastogne before the remainder of the 101st could be deployed. In fact, the commander of 2 Panzer Division, Oberst Meinrad von Lauchert, had suggested just this, but was ordered in no uncertain terms to press on to the river Meuse.

Lieutenant-Colonel Julian Ewell, CO of the 501st PIR at Bastogne, had commanded its 3rd Battalion on D-Day and at Eindhoven during Operation 'Market Garden' before taking over the regiment. He ended the war with the rank of major-general. (U.S. Army)

After conferring with VIII Corps' commander, Troy Middleton, and the 101st Airborne Division's acting CO, Brigadier-General Anthony McAuliffe, Colonel Ewell got the 501st PIR on the road at 0600 hrs on 19 December with Major Ray Bottomly's 1st Battalion in the van. Soon after daybreak the leading platoons closed in on the château just west of Neffe, from which could be heard intense small-arms fire and the chatter of heavier automatic weapons.

After the Germans had effectively broken Team 'Cherry's forces at Longvilly, a detachment from Panzer Lehr (after losing one tank to a bazooka round) had driven its reconnaissance platoon back from its roadblock near the railway station in Neffe to the stone-walled château. Stripping his vehicles of their .50 machine-guns and mounting them in the castle windows, Colonel Cherry and his tiny garrison had held out for four hours before the paras' timely arrival. Later in the day, however, incendiaries set the château ablaze and it had to be evacuated, the survivors falling back to Mont.

The only other troops left defending the Neffe–Bizory line were some engineers from Sam Tabets' 158th Battalion on the left and Lieutenant-Colonel Paul Symbol's 35th on the right. Colonel Ewell wasted no time rectifying the situation but it was fortunate that Panzer Lehr did not pursue its advantage. (The division's commander, Generalleutnant Fritz Bayerlein, confessed after the war that the unexpected opposition east of Bastogne had caused him a temporary loss of nerve.)

Positioning Bottomly's I/501st in the centre of his line, Ewell sent the second battalion to arrive, Homan's II/501st, towards Bizory, and positioned Lieutenant-Colonel George Griswold's III/501st on his right with orders to secure Mont and the ridge south of Neffe. Griswold's Company I was on the far right of the

16/12/1944	17/12	18/12	19/12	20/12	21/12	22/12	23/12	24/12	25/12	26/12	27/12	28/12	29/12
pages 66-72	77-78	73-76	81-82,85-86	27-34,83-84	87-88,94-95	39-40		35-38,89-90					

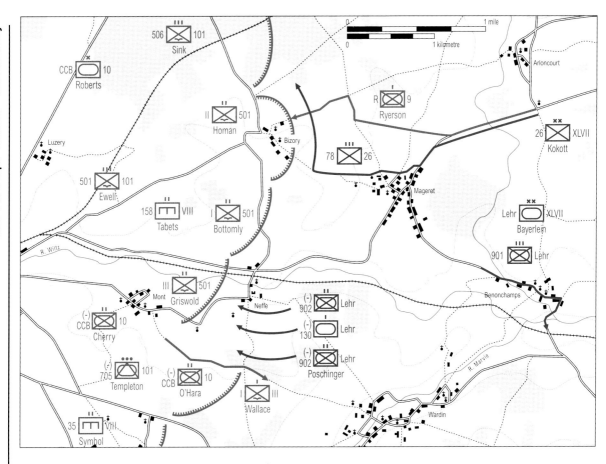

Although 902 Panzergrenadier Regiment forced the defenders out of Neffe, the arrival of the 501st Parachute Infantry Regiment securely blocked eastern access to Bastogne, forcing Panzer Lehr to detour southwest.

line at Wardin, where it had a tough fight before establishing contact with CCB/10th's Team 'O'Hara'.

In the centre of the line between Neffe and Bizory, the enemy remained strangely silent, although further east Panzer Lehr was busy destroying what remained of CCR/9th and Ryerson's task force between Longvilly and Mageret. At Bizory, on the left flank, 26 Volksgrenadier Division's 78th Regiment tried probing towards Luzery, intending to get into Bastogne down the Noville road. The grenadiers, already exhausted from trying to keep up with the Panzer divisions, came under heavy flanking fire from II/501st's Company F, forcing them to veer north, using the woods as cover. Meanwhile, all along the line the paras extended the foxholes already dug by the combat engineers and waited for the onslaught.

Panzer Lehr attacked during the night of the 19th, two battalions of 902 Panzergrenadier Regiment supported by a company of tanks moving against III/501st south of Neffe. Colonel Ewell called down artillery fire while Griswold's paras, well dug-in on the ridge east of Mont, poured a withering hail of fire into the ranks of the grenadiers, who were literally hamstrung by Belgian farmers' barbed wire fences. Flares fired by a platoon of M18s from Lieutenant-Colonel Cliff Templeton's 705th Tank Destroyer Battalion outside Marvie illuminated the scene, and after three Panzers had been destroyed, the rest retired with the infantry following. It had, in truth, been a half-hearted attack because by this time Bayerlein had decided the best way into Bastogne was from the south and west. For the time being, therefore, Ewell's 501st would be left in peace. By 21 December, however, Bastogne was completely encircled and the siege began in earnest. However, Patton's 4th Armored Division was on its way ...

16/12/1944	17/12	18/12	19/12	20/12	21/12	22/12	23/12	24/12	25/12	26/12	27/12	28/12	29/12
pages 66-72	77-78	73-76	81-82,85-86	27-34,83-84	87-88,94-95	39-40		35-38,89-90					

U.S. VIII CORPS' BATTLES

Team 'O'Hara', Company I, III/501st Parachute Infantry Regiment and 705th Tank Destroyer Battalion

Wardin/Marvie – December 19–20

Lieutenant-Colonel Clifford Templeton's 705th Tank Destroyer Battalion, activated a week after the Japanese attack on Pearl Harbor in December 1941 and shipped to France in July 1944, deserves a bigger part in the story of the 'Battle of the Bulge' than it usually receives. Transferred from Ninth Army and ordered to Bastogne on 18 December 1944, its commander dropped off eight M18s at Ortheuville en route which had a significant effect on the speed of the German LVIII Korps' advance. So did the battalion's lightly armoured but fast-moving 'Hellcat' tank destroyers in the ensuing battle around Bastogne itself after they arrived during the evening of 19 December, just in time to help repel Panzer Lehr south of Neffe and play a part in the battles for Noville and Champs to the northeast and west.

Abandoned but still looking defiant, one of the Team 'O'Hara' M4s beside the road between Wardin and Marvie after Panzer Lehr struck out at the threat to its southern flank. (U.S. Signal Corps)

Before the arrival of the 705th, and the 101st Airborne, the defence on the southeastern flank of Bastogne rested almost solely with the second of 10th Armored Division Combat Command B's task forces, Team 'O'Hara'. Commanded by Lieutenant-Colonel James O'Hara, CO of the 54th Armored Infantry Battalion, this comprised Company B of the 54th; the M4s of Company C, 21st Tank Battalion; a platoon of M5s from Company D of the 3rd Tank Battalion; a platoon of engineers; and a cavalry platoon. O'Hara had a 'watching brief' on the villages of Wardin and Marvie on the south bank of the river Wiltz, overlooking the main Diekirch–Ettelbruck–Eschdorf road. His men therefore had a predominantly quiet day on the 19th, because the main German forces were north of the river, heading west from Wiltz and Clervaux through the tatters of the 110th Regiment, 28th Infantry Division.

The first O'Hara's men knew of any Germans in their immediate vicinity was when a Jeep driven by Company C commander Lieutenant John Devereaux

16/12/1944	17/12	18/12	19/12	20/12	21/12	22/12	23/12	24/12	25/12	26/12	27/12	28/12	29/12
pages 66-72	77-78	73-76	79-80,85-86	27-34,83-84	87-88,94-95	39-40		35-38,89-90					

was fired on just outside Wardin. Even as he hastily reversed, paras of Company I, III/501st, started entering the village from the northwest, unseen in the thick morning mist. Part of Panzer Lehr's reconnaissance battalion moved in from the northeast at the same time, and the two groups inevitably collided in the middle. The 130-odd men of Captain Claude Wallace's company made a brave effort of it, fighting from house to house and disabling a Jagdpanzer IV with a bazooka round. But the paras were quickly overwhelmed, losing all their officers including Wallace amongst the 45 killed or badly wounded, and the survivors retreated southwest towards Marvie, past O'Hara's position on the wooded hill overlooking the highway. Like so many small-scale actions in the Ardennes, the whole tragic skirmish had been more of

Lieutenant-Colonel James O'Hara's blocking position outside Wardin, on the flank of Panzer Lehr's westward route, forced the bulk of the division to take a more southerly road, leaving just one regiment behind.

an accident than a planned move. Bayerlein had no interest in Wardin until American troops moved in. Then it became a potential threat to his southern flank and an obstacle to his drive towards the Meuse.

The next attack towards O'Hara's position started at about 0645 hrs on 20 December with an artillery barrage which brought a prompt response from the supporting 420th Field Artillery Battalion. Neither side could actually see what they were firing at because it was foggy again, so there was little damage. As the weak wintry sun began to disperse the mist, a Jagdpanzer IV opened up, seeming to aim directly at O'Hara's command post. It was actually firing at some of his M5s outside Marvie! Then, as more German tanks and infantry half-tracks of 901 Panzergrenadier Regiment appeared, heading west, O'Hara's M4s had a field day; two shots disposed of two Panzers, a bazooka round got a third and the fourth fled. The Jagdpanzer also tried to turn back, but was hit and burst into flames. The battle of Wardin was over, but that for Marvie had only just begun.

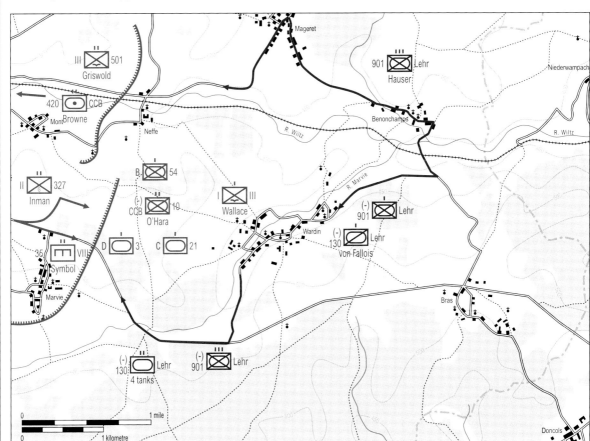

16/12/1944	17/12	18/12	19/12	20/12	21/12	22/12	23/12	24/12	25/12	26/12	27/12	28/12	29/12
pages 66-72	77-78	73-76	79-80,85-86	27-34,83-84	87-88,94-95	39-40		35-38,89-90					

U.S. VIII CORPS' BATTLES

II/327th Glider Infantry Regiment, 101st Airborne Division

Marvie – December 20–24

'**N**uts!' The story of the German surrender demand to the Bastogne garrison, and Brigadier-General Anthony McAuliffe's reply, has been repeated and embellished so many times that it will not be reiterated here. It would not have been included at all apart for the facts that the German emissaries delivered their ultimatum into the lines of Lieutenant-Colonel Roy Inman's 2nd Battalion of the 327th Glider Infantry Regiment (II/327th GIR) at 1130 hrs on 22 December; and that it was the regiment's CO, Colonel Joseph Harper, who returned with McAuliffe's reply and his own translation, 'Go to Hell!' Forever afterwards, he could not understand why he added, 'And good luck'.

Inman's battalion relieved Company A of the 35th Engineer Combat Battalion just west of Marvie at the same time in the morning of 20 December that Panzer Lehr inadvisably launched its four tanks, solitary Jagdpanzer and a company of infantry against the Team 'O'Hara' M5s, with the result already described. However, Inman himself was wounded by an HE round from one of the German Panzers. In the meanwhile, half a dozen half-tracks had sped ahead of the tanks and deposited the company of 901 Panzergrenadier Regiment right in the middle of the little village.

Inman's executive officer, Major R.B. Galbreaith, took charge and organised a counter-attack. Whether it was the paras' ferocity, or German lack of the same quality in this instance, which counted most in the hand-to-hand fighting which followed is impossible to say, but the result by 1300 hrs was 30 German dead to five Americans. The rest of the Panzergrenadiers either fled or were taken prisoner. Marvie now belonged to II/327th and, for the rest of the day, they were mercifully left alone to consolidate their hard-earned gains.

During 20 December the bulk of 2 Panzer Division to the north and Panzer Lehr to the south bypassed Bastogne in their westward drive towards the river Meuse, but 26 Volksgrenadier Division was tightening its hold on the perimeter and would soon be reinforced. By midnight all roads in and out of the town were closed, and Troy Middleton entrusted McAuliffe with command of all the troops within the ravelins of the surrounding villages. To put that in perspective, Bastogne was a 'fortress' with a curtain wall roughly two and a half miles (4 km) in diameter. At Marvie and the other outposts, this was of little concern. The night had turned bitterly cold and snow flurries were beginning to drift. The battle had become a pure one of endurance and survival.

Fortunately for II/327th GIR the next two days passed almost without incident, apart from some shelling and the surrender demand on the 22nd. Many of the paras seriously believed that the *Germans* were offering to surrender, and started relaxing. They knew that Patton's Third Army was on its way, so maybe the 'krauts' did too!

The daylight hours of 23 December also passed without major incident apart from the waves of C-47 Skytrains which began parachuting in food, medical supplies and ammunition now that the skies had fi-nally cleared. The airlift would last for six days and include Waco gliders carrying heavier Christmas 'goodies' – especially shells for the artillery and fuel for the tanks. But there was still no sign of Patton, and II/327th's delusion that the ordeal was nearly over was rudely shattered at 1725 hrs when concentrated shellfire began landing on Marvie.

Having advanced west, chasing 2 Panzer Division, the commander of Panzer Lehr, General Bayerlein, had left behind his 901 Panzergrenadier Regiment reinforced by Kompanie 6 from the Panzer Abteilung.

16/12/1944	17/12	18/12	19/12	20/12	21/12	22/12	23/12	24/12	25/12	26/12	27/12	28/12	29/12
pages 66-72	77-78	73-76	79-82,85-86	27-34	87-88,94-95	39-40		35-38,89-90					

The shellfire came from these tanks, and some self-propelled guns, hidden behind a crest in the woods southeast of the village. Then came the German infantry, stealthily to begin with, hoping to catch the battalion's outlying platoons unawares, and one indeed was soon surrounded. Colonel O'Hara sent an M15 half-track to their assistance, but there were four German tanks in the way. The half-track driver hared back into Marvie, where the men of the 327th, thinking the vehicle German, blew it to bits. But it blocked the road for the following real German vehicles. Not so their infantry, who by 2000 hrs were into the south side of Marvie and working their way from house to house.

The German attacks at Marvie, designed to give them entry into Bastogne from the southwest, were only narrowly beaten off by II/327th Glider Infantry Regiment and Team 'O'Hara'.

Now, the Panzers started infiltrating on the II/327th's right flank. About a dozen attacked Company F but were stopped by O'Hara's M4s and Templeton's M18s. Another pair of O'Hara's Shermans, braving the Panzerfausts, ventured into Marvie itself. They knocked out one Panzer when it ran into the accidental roadblock, which helped stabilise the situation somewhat although the infantry battle continued.

By this time it was the morning of Christmas Eve. Colonel 'Bud' Harper, who had assumed personal command of the battle, could still not relax, though. The second assault against Marvie had been contained and at least eight German tanks destroyed. The II/327th GIR's line was dented but not broken. However, Harper and his men knew they could not hold out forever like this, and the question in all their minds was, 'Where's Patton?' They were not alone in their anxiety, because the Bastogne perimeter was under threat at every point.

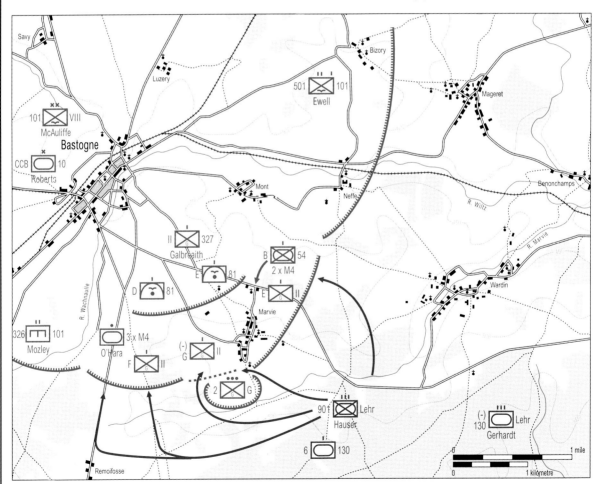

16/12/1944	17/12	18/12	19/12	20/12	21/12	22/12	23/12	24/12	25/12	26/12	27/12	28/12	29/12
pages 66-72	77-78	73-76	79-82,85-86	27-34	87-88,94-95	39-40		35-38,89-90					

U.S. VIII CORPS' BATTLES

Team 'Desobry' and I/506th Parachute Infantry Regiment, 101st Airborne Division

Noville – December 19–20

The two-day battle for Noville, north and slightly east of Bastogne on the Houffalize road, was costly, but had the effect of so delaying 2 Panzer Division that, by the time it reached the Meuse, 2nd Armored Division was there to greet it.

Noville was the third village assigned by Middleton to Colonel William Roberts' CCB, 10th Armored Division, and the team sent there under Major William Desobry (CO of 20th Armored Infantry Battalion) included a company of 15 M4s from the 3rd Tank Battalion and a platoon of four M18s from the 609th Tank Destroyer Battalion. They arrived in Noville at about 2300 hrs on 18 December and six hours later had no problem deterring a German reconnaissance patrol scouting westward from Bourcy. What they did not realise was that this was merely the vanguard of the entire 2 Panzer Division, which was in a hurry after having already been held up by CCR, 9th Armored Division, and Team 'Cherry' on the Longvilly road.

The main German assault began at 1030 hrs on 19 December. The German commander, Oberst Meinrad von Lauchert, had brought up almost the whole of 3 Panzer Regiment supported by most of the division's self-propelled artillery pieces. As the fog which had obscured the battlefield suddenly lifted, all Desobry's men in the roadblocks on the Vaux and Houffalize roads could see was tanks, at least 30 of them. Artillery fire crashed into Noville as the Panzers clattered forward. Nine were knocked out by Desobry's M4s and M18s at ranges of between 1,000 and 200 yards but two got into Noville itself. One was destroyed by a Sherman at 75 yards range and the second by an M7 at 30 yards!

The battle lasted about an hour before the Germans withdrew to rethink, but Desobry had only eight Shermans left and knew he could not withstand a second similar assault, so asked for permission to withdraw to the high ground at Foy. Colonel Roberts

Men of Lieutenant-Colonel James LaPrade's I/506th Parachute Infantry Regiment march north out of Bastogne on the morning of 19 December towards Noville, past an M3 half-track and 105mm M7 GMC of Colonel William Roberts' CCB, 10th Armored Division. (U.S. Army)

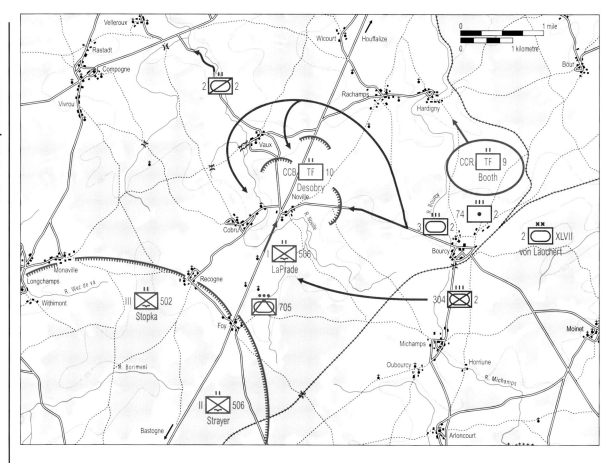

Major William Desobry's spirited defence at Noville held up 2 Panzer Division's advance to the Meuse for a vital 24 hours which resulted in their almost total defeat at Celles five days later.

told him to use his own judgement, but advised him that a battalion of paras and a platoon of tank destroyers from the 705th Battalion were on their way.

Lieutenant-Colonel James LaPrade's I/506th PIR began arriving at about midday, warmly welcomed by the German artillery. The main problem the defenders faced was that the Germans occupied the high ground around Noville, so by 1430 hrs LaPrade had organised his paras for a counter-attack towards the northeast. One of his assault companies ran into a hail of fire and was stopped cold with heavy casualties, but the other two reached the ridge. From there they could count 32 Panzers forming up for another attack. The surprise on both sides was complete, and the German tanks, apparently fearful of bazookas, contented themselves with firing from long range. The paras fell back towards

Noville, and both sides afterwards claimed that they had halted enemy counter-attacks!

As the short day drew to a close, the Germans contented themselves with shelling the village. LaPrade was killed during the night and Desobry badly wounded, their places being taken respectively by Majors Robert Harwick and Charles Hustead. Harwick assumed overall command.

Von Lauchert resumed his attack at 0530 hrs on 20 December, this time deploying his tanks in small packets each accompanied by grenadiers. Artillery fire from batteries northwest of Bastogne caused casualties among the German infantry but did not dent the tanks. The problem was that Hustead's Shermans had run out of armour-piercing ammunition, and by mid-morning Harwick had to report to Roberts, 'Situation critical.' By this time, however, II/506th and III/502nd PIRs occupied good positions either side of Foy and, using the swirling fog and smoke as cover, Harwick's paras and Hustead's remaining tanks were able to fight their way back to safety.

16/12/1944	17/12	18/12	19/12	20/12	21/12	22/12	23/12	24/12	25/12	26/12	27/12	28/12	29/12
pages 66-72	77-78	73-76	79-82	27-34,83-84	87-88,94-95	39-40		35-38,89-90					

U.S. VIII CORPS' BATTLES

I/401st (III/327th) Glider Infantry Regiment, 101st Airborne Division

Flamierge/Hemroulle – December 21–25

After being ignominiously transported to Bastogne by truck, these were a sight for sore eyes to the men of the 327th. Sixty Waco CG-4A gliders took part in the Bastogne airlift, 42 of them landing safely within the perimeter. Amongst their heavier loads were fuel drums and 155mm shells. (U.S. Army)

Although carried in the books as the 3rd Battalion of the 327th Glider Infantry Regiment, the men of Lieutenant-Colonel Ray Allen's command still regarded themselves as the 1st Battalion of the 401st, having fought as such in Normandy and Holland before being assigned to their sister regiment on 28 November 1944. The last battalion of the 101st Airborne to arrive in the Ardennes, I/401st was given the job of guarding the 'back door' into Bastogne west of Mande-St Étienne. The battalion was actually out on quite a limb with a wide gap between its own left and the right flank of I/327th at Senochamps, and between its right and the left flank of the 502nd PIR at Champs. Thus, although the battalion had a relatively quiet time at the beginning of the siege, there was no 'peace on earth' this Christmas.

Even before the German attacks began in earnest, Colonel Allen had carefully planned a line of retreat to shorten the line and secure his flanks. He was very conscious of the fact that the bulk of the Bastogne garrison's 105 and 155mm artillery pieces were concentrated behind him in a circle just west of the town. Allen planned that Company C, furthest west guarding the main road to Marche and St Hubert, would fall back through Company B at Flamizoulle, join up with Company A near Champs and form the battalion reserve for a new line in front of Hemroulle. In the light of subsequent events, it was as well that Allen was so farsighted.

On 23 December he was forced to pull Company C back from Flamierge and established a new line just west of Champs and Grandes-Fanges. To the battalion's south, Mande-St Étienne was also abandoned, closing the gap between the I/401st, I/327th and Team 'Roberts', defending the artillery. However, the reconnaissance battalion of 26 Volksgrenadier Division moved into the vacated area, closing the net around Bastogne still more tightly.

Meanwhile, Hitler had authorised the release of two fresh divisions from reserve, 9 Panzer and the veteran

16/12/1944		17/12	18/12		19/12	20/12		21/12		22/12	23/12	24/12	25/12	26/12	27/12	28/12	29/12
pages 66-72		77-78	73-76		79-82,85-86	27-34,83-84		94-95		39-40		35-38,89-90					

87

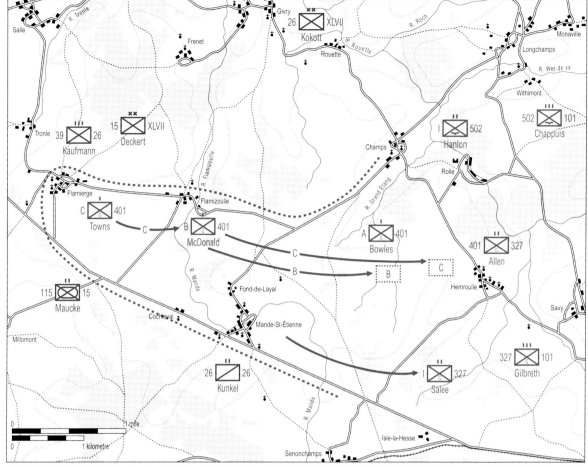

After falling back from Flamierge and Flamizoulle as planned, I/401st Glider Infantry Regiment was then assaulted west of Hemroulle, but Kampfgruppe 'Maucke' only got a few hundred yards further.

15 Panzergrenadier, which had earlier distinguished itself in North Africa and Italy. A reinforced battlegroup from the latter, Kampfgruppe 'Maucke', was assigned to the battle for Bastogne. Oberst Heinz Kokott, the scholarly 50-year-old CO of 26 Volksgrenadier Division in charge of co-ordinating the siege, moved the battlegroup into the line at Flamierge late on Christmas Eve. The 'big show' was about to begin.

At 0500 hrs on Christmas morning the commander of I/401st's Company A, 1st Lieutenant Howard Bowles, phoned Allen to say that 18 German tanks were approaching from east of Mande-St Étienne. The spearhead of Kampfgruppe 'Maucke' broke clear through between Company A and Captain Bob

McDonald's Company B, but the paras stayed in their foxholes to deal with the following grenadiers, capturing 92 of them – nearly half their own number of men. Then, at 0710 hrs Allen received a radio call from the commander of his reserve Company C, Captain Preston Towns. 'If you look out of your window,' he told Allen, 'you'll be looking right down the muzzle of an 88.' Allen hastily left through the back door of his command post! After reaching the lines of the 463rd Parachute Field Artillery Battalion, he continued to direct the battle by radio.

Amazingly, his men were still holding. Once it had broken through Companies A and B, the Panzer column had split, half heading towards Hemroulle and the rest north towards Champs, where they were dealt with by the 502nd PIR. Two of the tanks had been blown apart by tank destroyers from the 705th and Allen's infantry dealt with the remainder. Not one of the tanks or infantrymen from Kampfgruppe 'Maucke' returned to tell the tale.

16/12/1944	17/12	18/12	19/12	20/12	21/12	22/12	23/12	24/12	25/12	26/12	27/12	28/12	29/12
pages 66-72	77-78	73-76	79-82,85-86	27-34,83-84	94-95	39-40		35-38,89-90					

U.S. VIII CORPS' BATTLES

I/ and II/502nd Parachute Infantry Regiment, 101st Airborne Division

Champs/Longchamps – December 24–25

It was Christmas Eve in the Château Rolle. Many of the officers of Lieutenant-Colonel Steve Chappuis' 502nd PIR celebrated Mass in the 10th-century chapel. It was a time for prayer, and all the combat diaries of those locked inside the Bastogne perimeter show the same sense of unease that the lack of enemy aggression during the day boded ill for the morrow. 'For the first time all around the perimeter men felt fearful,' recorded Colonel (later Brigadier-General) Sam Marshall. 'It seemed to them that the end was at hand. That night many of them shook hands with their comrades.' The sombre feeling of nostalgia was shared in the German lines, and the carol 'Heilige Nacht' seemed more than usually poignant.

The fears of all the men on both sides were justified because daybreak saw the beginning of the last major German attack on Bastogne before the belated arrival of Patton's 4th Armored Division on Boxing Day. General Heinrich von Lüttwitz had ordered that the town finally be taken. The main effort was to be made by the 77th Regiment of Oberst Heinz Kokott's 26 Volksgrenadier Division from Givry towards Champs, with the newly arrived 115Panzergrenadier Regiment (Kampfgruppe 'Maucke') on its right towards Hem-roulle. Opposing them between Champs and Long-champs was Major John Hanlon's I/502nd PIR, with Colonel Allen's I/401st GIR holding the line to his southwest and Lieutenant-Colonel Tom Sutcliffe's II/502nd on his right.

The first assault by 77 Volksgrenadier Regiment hit

PzKpfw IV from Kampfgruppe 'Maucke', probably destroyed by an M18 from the 705th Tank Destroyer Battalion in between Hemroulle and Champs on Christmas morning. Not a single one of the tanks from 115 Panzer Abteilung survived the battle. The 502nd PIR's CO, Colonel Chappuis, was awarded the Distinguished Service Cross for his action here. (U.S. Army)

16/12/1944	17/12	18/12	19/12	20/12	21/12	22/12	23/12	24/12	25/12	26/12	27/12	28/12	29/12
pages 66-72	77-78	73-76	79-82,85-86	27-34,83-84	87-88,94-95	39-40		35-38					

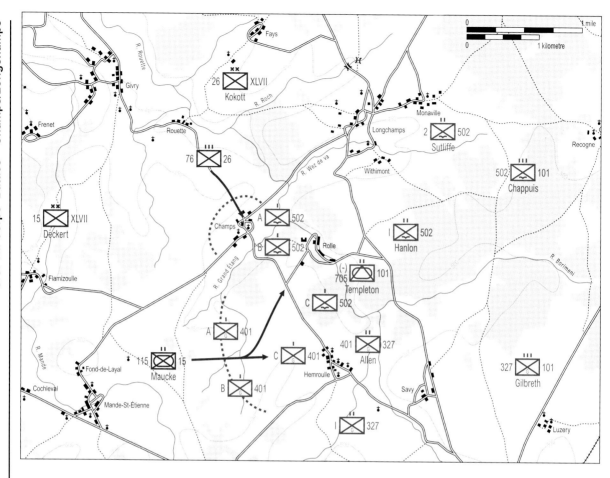

While Company A battled against the assault troops of 77 Volksgrenadier Division the other forces engaged made short work of Kampfgruppe 'Maucke'.

Hanlon's Company A just northwest of Champs at 0330 hrs after a half-hour artillery barrage. By 0400 the grenadiers were into the village itself and a fierce hand-to-hand battle was raging. Chappuis ordered Hanlon to move Company B from Hemroulle to establish a roadblock south of Champs, but not to get engaged in the fight until there was enough light to distinguish friend from foe. Meanwhile, another battalion of grenadiers had infiltrated the woods west of Longchamps and engaged Sutcliffe's Company E.

The next bad news was that tanks had penetrated the lines of I/401st and that a group of seven, accompanied by about a battalion of infantry, was heading straight towards the regimental command post in the Château Rolle. All the men in the castle, including the walking wounded, grabbed their

weapons and took up positions on the high ground overlooking the road to the west, leaving just Colonel Chappuis with his deputy, Lieutenant-Colonel Patrick Cassidy, and a radio operator in the château. Chappuis alerted Hanlon to the threat to Company B's rear and told him to bring Company C north in support.

The company joined two M18s of the 705th Tank Destroyer Battalion on the edge of the wood just south of Rolle. Their machine-gun and rifle fire swept the German tanks clear of the grenadiers who had been riding on them, and the Panzers veered left towards Champs, where Company A was still hanging on by the skin of its teeth. This manoeuvre exposed the PzKpfw IVs' more thinly armoured flanks to Templeton's M18s and three succumbed instantly to well-aimed shots. Bazookas got two more. The brave crew of one tank got into Champs before being hit from all sides, while the more prudent crew of the seventh abandoned their vehicle and surrendered. Apart from mopping up, it was the end of the battle.

16/12/1944	17/12	18/12	19/12	20/12	21/12	22/12	23/12	24/12	25/12	26/12	27/12	28/12	29/12
pages 66-72	77-78	73-76	79-82,85-86	27-34,83-84	87-88,94-95	39-40		35-38					

BRITISH 21st ARMY GROUP

BRITISH XXX CORPS

At the beginning of December 1944, Lieutenant-General Brian Horrocks' XXX Corps was fighting in the bogs and swamps of southwest Holland, attacking alongside the U.S. 84th Infantry

Lieutenant-General (later, Sir) Brian Horrocks was an old-style cavalryman. When he heard the Germans were approaching Bruxelles, he wanted to carry on so that XXX Corps could fight them at Waterloo!
(Imperial War Museum)

Division towards Geilenkirchen. Its adversary was General der Panzertruppen Heinrich Freiherr von Lüttwitz's XLVII Panzer Korps, which Horrocks' men would re-encounter at Christmas east of the river Meuse.

One of the first things that Field Marshal Bernard Law Montgomery did, as soon as Eisenhower had given him command of the U.S. First and Ninth Armies, was promise British support in halting the German Ardennes offensive. On the morning of 20 December, while news of the change in command was still being disseminated, a major from Montgomery's staff arrived at Courtney Hodges' First Army headquarters with news that at least took one worry off Hodges' shoulders. He was told that the field marshal was moving Horrocks' XXX Corps south from Holland into the Hasselt–Louvain–St Trond area to ensure that if any German spearheads did reach the Meuse, they would not get across.

The first units to move out would be the 29th and 33rd Armoured Brigades with Shermans, some of them Fireflies, followed by the 34th Army Tank Brigade with heavily armoured Churchills, then the

---

BRITISH XXX CORPS
Lieutenant-General Brian G. Horrocks

6 Airborne Division (Bols)
51 (Highland) Infantry Division (Rennie)
53 (Welsh) Infantry Division (Ross)
29 Armoured Brigade (Harvey)
33 Armoured Brigade (Scott)
34 Army Tank Brigade (Clarke)
2 Household Cavalry Regiment
11 Hussars & Cavalry Regiment
53 Reconnaissance Regiment
61 Reconnaissance Regiment
73 Antitank Regiment
4 Royal Horse Artillery Regiment (25pdr)
5 Royal Horse Artillery Regiment (25pdr)
7 Royal Artillery Regiment (5.5")
64 Royal Artillery Regiment (5.5")
84 Royal Artillery Regiment (5.5")
106 Anti-Aircraft Brigade (3.7" & 40mm)
27 Light Anti-Aircraft Regiment (40mm)
Special Air Service Squadron (Belgian)
16 & 30 Bataillons Chasseurs (-), 2 Régiment Parachutistes
  (Puech-Samson) (French) (attached to U.S. Third Army
  21 December as liaison between British 6 Airborne and
  U.S. 87 Infantry Divisions)
Corps Reserve:
43 (Wessex) Infantry Division (Thomas)
Guards Armoured Division (Adair)

Guards Armoured Division and the 43rd, 51st and 53rd Infantry Divisions. In particular, Hodges was told, the British would assume responsibility for safeguarding the Meuse crossing points at Liège, Namur, Huy and Givet. In his memoirs, Montgomery was later to write that, at this stage, there was 'little to prevent German armoured cars and reconnaissance elements [from] bounding the Meuse and advancing on Brussels'. British troops accordingly began setting

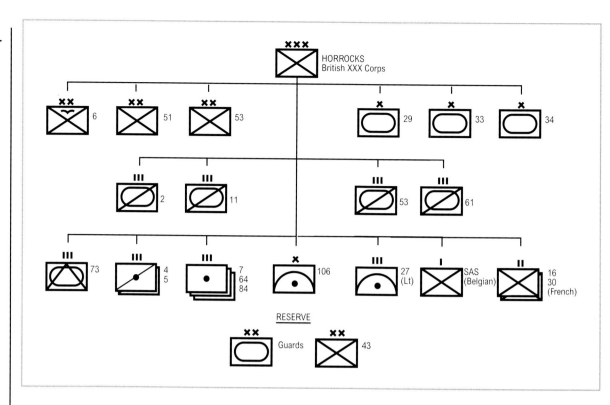

up hasty roadblocks to protect the Belgian capital while others began moving towards Liège.

Apart from the 29th Armoured Brigade, British forces saw little action until the counter-offensive began in earnest on 3 January 1945. By then XXX Corps had moved up to the vicinity of Marche, joined just after Christmas by the 6th Airborne Division, which took over the lines of the U.S. 84th Infantry

British Shermans, believed to be from the 23rd Hussars, 29th Armoured Brigade, near Rochefort in January 1945. (Imperial War Museum)

Division. This put it on the right (southern) flank of the British line, with the 53rd (Welsh) Division on the left. The 53rd cleared the area south of Marche and reached La Roche, where the division was opposed by 116 Panzer Division, which counter-attacked several times. The 51st (Highland) Division now took the lead and finally captured La Roche on 11 January.

On XXX Corps' right, 6th Airborne supported by the 23rd Hussars from 29th Armoured Brigade had to battle against Panzer Lehr at Bures over 3-4 January. Casualties were heavy, and the driver of one stretcher Jeep, Sergeant Scott from the Hussars, might easily have become another when a Jagdpanther from 559 schwere Panzerjäger Abteilung rounded a corner in the village. Instead, the unknown German commander told the medic, 'Take the wounded away this time, but don't come back. It's not safe.'

This individual act of chivalry turned sour afterwards when men of the 6th Airborne's 9th Parachute Battalion discovered the bodies of the menfolk from the little village of Bande lying in a heap, all shot through the back of the head. By this stage of the war, most British soldiers were hardened veterans well used to most of war's brutalities, but a sight like this – not uncommon in the Ardennes – sickened them all. However, they were not to stay long because on 16 January, once the U.S. First and Third Armies were reunited at Houffalize, Montgomery began withdrawing XXX Corps to rejoin 21st Army Group in Holland.

29th Armoured Brigade

The men of the 29th Armoured Brigade had been looking forward to spending Christmas in Bruxelles when news of the German offensive reached them. After the mauling they had received during the battle for Caen in the summer, and the miles they had driven in the subsequent pursuit, men and vehicles were both tired out. In fact, at the beginning of December the three tank regiments had been ordered back from Holland to turn their Shermans over to the Armoured Replacement Group outside the capital and await delivery of the new Comet tanks, of which they were to be the first recipients.

A British armoured 'regiment' in fact equated approximately to an American or German battalion, with 666 officers and men, 61 Shermans and 11 light tanks. The 29th Armoured Brigade's three armoured regiments (3rd Royal Tanks, 23rd Hussars and 2nd Fife & Forfar) were supported by a reinforced motorised infantry regiment, the 8th Rifle Brigade, with a nominal complement of 818 officers and men. In fact, in December 1944, manpower was seriously down after six months of continuous fighting and only 50 of the brigade's Shermans were serviceable.

After suffering heavy casualties during Operations 'Epsom' and 'Goodwood' in the summer, even though they did result in the capture of Caen, Brigadier

29th ARMOURED BRIGADE
Brigadier C. B. C. Harvey
HQ Company
2 Fife & Forfar Yeomanry
3 Royal Tank Regiment (Brown)
23 Hussars
8 Rifle Brigade

Harvey's men reckoned they were in for another 'shambles' when, instead of collecting their new Comet tanks after a relaxing Christmas, they were ordered to retrieve their old Shermans, get them running again and move east to the Meuse. Colonel Alan Brown's 3rd Royal Tank Regiment went to Dinant and reaped all the glory for halting 2 Panzer Division's reconnaissance battalion at Foy-Notre-Dame, while the 23rd Hussars and 2nd Fife & Forfar Yeomanry Regiments guarded the Meuse river crossings at Givet and Namur, before joining in the counter-offensive in January 1945.

Once back in Holland, 29th Armoured Brigade did finally receive its new Comet tanks and ended the war in Germany.

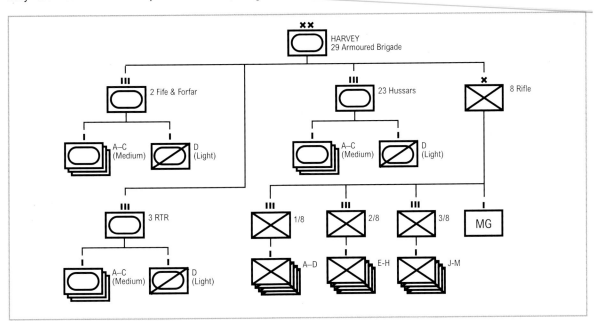

BRITISH XXX CORPS' BATTLE
3rd Royal Tank Regiment

Dinant/Foy-Notre-Dame – December 21–26

At 0200 hrs on Wednesday 21 December the duty officer of 29th Armoured Brigade, 11th Armoured Division, received a phone call from Montgomery's 21st Army Group headquarters in Holland telling him to waste no time getting the brigade moving. After picking up the serviceable vehicles from among their discarded Shermans at the replacement depot outside Bruxelles, and putting fuel, food and ammunition on board, the brigade had a squadron of tanks apiece at Namur, Dinant and Givet by 1630 hrs.

At Dinant, Colonel Alan Brown, CO of 3rd Royal Tank Regiment, got the supporting company of

Sherman Fireflies (this vehicle is actually from the Fife & Forfar Yeomanry at Namur) with high-velocity 17 pdr guns were the most effective tanks the Western Allies possessed. (U.S. Army)

infantry from 8th Rifle Brigade to laying mines on the approaches to the crucial bridge over the Meuse and, retaining the bulk of his battalion west of the river, put a troop of M4s on the other side. One tank was positioned to guard each of the roads from the east. Theirs was not quite a suicide mission, although the crews knew they were not expected to return with their tanks, but to leave their hulks as roadblocks.

Lacking any hard intelligence regarding German forces or dispositions, 3 RTR's first encounter with the enemy came as a shock. A Jeep manned by three Germans with American greatcoats over their uniforms was blown to pieces on a mine. They were part of Otto Skorzeny's Operation 'Greif' kommando.

The second encounter was a different kind of shock, because the crew of a dug-in Sherman had fallen asleep during the night of 23 December, and

16/12/1944	17/12	18/12	19/12	20/12	21/12	22/12	23/12	24/12	25/12	26/12	27/12	28/12	29/12
pages 66-72	77-78	73-76	79-82,85-86	27-34,83-84	87-88,	39-40		35-38,89-90					

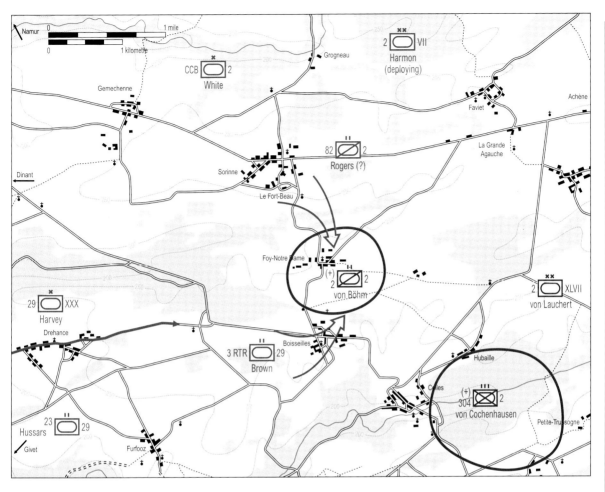

After repulsing one attempt by Kampfgruppe 'von Böhm' to cross the Meuse at Dinant, 3 RTR bounced back and counter-attacked alongside the 82nd Armored Reconnaissance Battalion at Foy, capturing von Böhm himself and 147 of his men.

only woke up at the sound of engines and tank tracks as Kampfgruppe 'von Böhm' headed for Dinant. The half-awake gunner's first shot blew up an ammunition truck and his second a PzKpfw IV, before the arrival of 'a self-propelled 88mm' (probably in reality a Jagdpanzer IV, because 2 Panzer Division had no Jagdpanthers) caused the crew prudently to retire.

Other individual 3 RTR Shermans knocked out another PzKpfw IV and two Panthers that night, convincing von Böhm that he would have to wait for reinforcements. Dinant was safe, and the 'death or glory' boys had postponed their final reckoning. It was now time to take the battle to the enemy.

At dawn on Christmas Day Alan Brown led the battalion forward in two columns, driving a German picket out of Boiselles before reaching Foy-Notre-Dame on the flank of the U.S. 82nd Armored Reconnaissance Battalion. Although they were met with a brief flurry of fire, the battle was soon over and most of Kampfgruppe 'von Böhm' went 'in the bag'. 3 RTR now moved to the ridge west of Celles, from which they had a grandstand view as 2nd Armored Division swept through the village, supported by swarms of fighter-bombers. An over-enthusiastic P-38 pilot strafed the British column, but fortunately there was only one casualty. The rest of 29th Armoured Brigade had also moved east by this time and, reunited, it took its place alongside 6th Airborne paras on the right of First Army, clearing St Hubert after a costly six-day battle at the beginning of January and linking up with men of Third Army's 87th Infantry Division on 11 January 1945.

16/12/1944	17/12	18/12	19/12	20/12	21/12	22/12	23/12	24/12	25/12	26/12	27/12	28/12	29/12
pages 66-72	77-78	73-76	79-82,85-86	27-34,83-84	87-88	39-40		35-38,89-90					

WARGAMING – THE ARDENNES
ALLIED CENTRAL SECTOR

The Ardennes Offensive of December '44 represents the last desperate gasp in the West by a defeated and crippled Germany. Recent anniversaries and commemorations, events in the cinema (as well as the reminiscences of relatives) have brought the war into sharper focus in the public mind with a consequent increase in interest. All these factors make World War II a must for many wargamers. Wargaming with model figures offers the budding general possibly the most visually satisfying medium for refighting World War II battles – particularly the Ardennes Campaign.

Figures and models
Below is a list, by no means comprehensive, of the main figure manufacturers. Many can be obtained from good model shops or the addresses of the individual manufacturers can be found in most wargamers magazines.
6-mm /1/300th Scale:
Heroics and Ross
1/285th Scale:
GHQ via Chiltern miniatures
10-mm/1/200th Scale:
Skytrex
Wargames South

15-mm Scale:
Skytrex
Old Glory
Tin Soldier
20-mm Scale:
SHQ
Skytrex
Platoon 20
Figures Armour and Artillery (FAA)
Wargames Foundry (limited ranges)
Plus many plastic kits by Matchbox, Airfix, Hasagawa, Esci etc …
25mm Scale:
1st Corps
Battle Honours

Computer Games
Empire Interactive's 'Battleground Ardennes'
Microsoft's 'Close Combat - Normandy to the Ardennes'
Strategic Simulation Inc's 'Panzer General'
Strategic Studies Group's 'Ardennes Offensive'

SELECT BIBLIOGRAPHY

Cole, Hugh M. *The Ardennes: Battle of the Bulge.* United States Army in World War II, Office of the Chief of Military History, Washington D.C., 1965.
Crookenden, Lieutenant-General Sir Napier. *Battle of the Bulge 1944.* Ian Allan, Shepperton, 1980.
Eisenhower, John S.D. *The Bitter Woods.* Robert Hale, London, 1969.
Elstob, Peter. *Hitler's Last Offensive,* Secker & Warburg, London, 1971.
MacDonald, Charles B. *The Battle of the Bulge.* George Weidenfeld & Nicolson, London, 1984.
Marshall, Colonel S.L.A. *Bastogne: The Story of the First Eight Days.* U.S. Army in action series, Center of Military History, Washington D.C., 1946, reprinted 1988.

Pallud, Jean Paul. *Battle of the Bulge Then and Now.* Battle of Britain Prints International, London, 1984.
Parker, Danny S. *Battle of the Bulge.* Greenhill Books, Lionel Leventhal Ltd, London, 1991.
Stanton, Shelby L. *World War II Order of Battle.* Presidio Press, Novato, California, 1984.
Quarrie, Bruce. *Airborne Assault.* Patrick Stephens, Wellingborough, 1991.
Strawson, John. *The Battle for the Ardennes.* B.T. Batsford, London, 1972.
Strong, Major-General Sir Kenneth. *Intelligence at the Top.* Cassell, London, 1968.

COMPANION SERIES FROM OSPREY

ELITE
Detailed information on the uniforms and insignia of the world's most famous military forces. Each 64-page book contains some 50 photographs and diagrams, and 12 pages of full-colour artwork.

NEW VANGUARD
Comprehensive histories of the design, development and operational use of the world's armoured vehicles and artillery. Each 48-page book contains eight pages of full-colour artwork including a detailed cutaway.

WARRIOR
Definitive analysis of the armour, weapons, tactics and motivation of the fighting men of history. Each 64-page book contains cutaways and exploded artwork of the warrior's weapons and armour.

CAMPAIGN
Concise, authoritative accounts of history's decisive military encounters. Each 96-page book contains over 90 illustrations including maps, orders of battle, colour plates, and three-dimensional battle maps.

MEN-AT-ARMS
An unrivalled source of information on the organisation, uniforms and equipment of the world's fighting men, past and present. The series covers hundreds of subjects spanning 5,000 years of history. Each 48-page book includes concise texts packed with specific information, some 40 photos, maps and diagrams, and eight colour plates of uniformed figures.

AIRCRAFT OF THE ACES
Focuses exclusively on the elite pilots of major air campaigns, and includes unique interviews with surviving aces sourced specifically for each volume. Each 96-page volume contains up to 40 specially commissioned artworks, unit listings, new scale plans and the best archival photography available.

COMBAT AIRCRAFT
Technical information from the world's leading aviation writers on the aircraft types flown. Each 96-page volume contains up to 40 specially commissioned artworks, unit listings, new scale plans and the best archival photography available.